Just for You...
Mum

Published in 2011 by Prion
An imprint of the Carlton Publishing Group
20 Mortimer Street
London WIT 3JW

10 9 8 7 6 5 4 3 2 1

A CIP catalogue record for this book is available from the British Library.

ISBN 978-1-85375-803-4

Printed and bound in the United Kingdom

M*Just for You...* um

Funny quotes, advice and stories for
your family's favourite person

Heather James

PRION

CONTENTS

INTRODUCTION

To her children, every mum is the centre of the world. She's
the one they run to when they fall out with a friend, cut their
knees or just need a hug. She's on hand to whip up a snack
when they're hungry, put them to bed when they're tired and
wipe their tears when they're upset.

The original multi-tasker, she can bathe the kids, vacuum the
house, answer her e-mails and cook dinner without smudging
her make-up. And she can light up the dullest of days with a
loving smile.

Every mother is unique, and each experience of motherhood
comes with its own particular package of trials, frustrations,
laughter and joy. However, some of the emotions, dilemmas
and heart-warming moments of mumdom are universal – and
are well worth sharing.

Just For You Mum is not an instruction manual, but a collection
of warm, delightful and amusing tales from women in the
know, including some 'Favourite Funnies' – jokes to prove that
mums everywhere can keep their sense of humour despite the
mayhem going on all around them!

Take a well-earned rest and delve into the experiences of
real mothers from pregnancy to the birth of grandchildren…
because, while no two mums are the same, we're all in this
together.

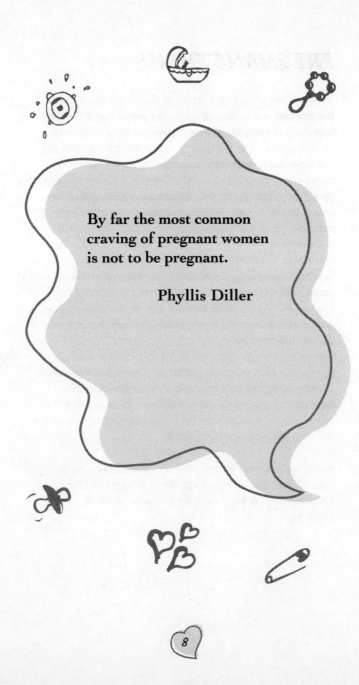

By far the most common craving of pregnant women is not to be pregnant.

Phyllis Diller

PREGNANT PAUSE

The trials and tribulations of pregnancy are as numerous (okay, maybe slightly more numerous) as the joys of carrying a child.

First time round pregnancy is, without doubt, the most life-changing event any woman will experience. But it also changes the lives of those around you, like the five-year-old who had been telling his teacher how excited he was about the baby brother or sister that he was soon to have.

One day, his mum let him feel her bulging tummy for signs of movement and the boy was obviously impressed, but made no comment.

When he stopped mentioning the baby in class, the teacher sat him down and asked, "Whatever has become of that baby brother or sister you were expecting at home?"

The boy burst into tears and confessed, "I think Mummy ate it!"

It is rare that one can see
in a little boy the promise
of a man, but one can
almost always see in a little
girl the threat of a woman.

Alexandre Dumas

You Bet!

On his TV show *You Bet Your Life*, Groucho Marx once interviewed a woman who had given birth to 22 children. "I love my husband," she said, by way of explanation. "I like my cigar, too," Groucho replied, "but I take it out once in a while."

Improperly practical

Roman statesman Marcus Vipsanius Agrippa had three sons and two daughters by his third wife Julia. However, her infidelity was legendary. When it was remarked upon, with some surprise, that all her children were the image of Agrippa, Julia explained; "That is because passengers are never allowed on board until the hold is full."

Biology lesson

Tina was thrilled when her aunt and uncle had their first child, and asked her mum where babies came from. Mum told her they came from mummy's tummy and explained how they got out, using the correct anatomical terms. A while later Tina's dad came into the room and, thrilled with her new knowledge, she jumped up and shouted, "Daddy, babies come from a China."

Life is tough enough without having someone kick you from the inside.

Rita Rudner

The joys of pregnancy

A word of warning on what to expect when you're expecting.

- Men will NOT stand up and give you their seat on the tube, train or bus, for fear that you are just overweight.

- The Jimmy Choos are out – not only will your ankles resemble balloons at the end of the day but your feet grow two sizes.

- You will never want to be more than five minutes away from the loo.

- People you barely know will stop you in the street to have a good feel of your stomach.

- Helpful friends will inundate you with horrific birth stories.

- Absolutely anything – from soppy movies to not being able to get the top off a jam jar – will make you cry.

- Your usually active brain will turn to mush.

- Your social life needn't suffer, as long as you can still be in bed by 9.30. Anything after that and you'll feel less like Cinderella and more like you've turned into a pumpkin.

- You'll realise how stupid everyone is when they're drunk.

Somewhere on this globe, every ten seconds, there is a woman giving birth to a child. She must be found and stopped.

Sam Levenson

Weird celebrity baby names

Most celebrities claim that they want to shield their children from the horrors of fame. However, that admirable intention is often overridden, it seems, by the compulsive desire to give their children names that will, at best, stand out on a school register and, at worst, make them a laughing stock.

Here are some of the more unusual names that celebs have chosen for their poor unsuspecting kids.

Nicolas Cage – Kal-El
Nic changed his own name to Cage in honour of comic book hero Luke Cage. He went one step further with his son, giving him Superman's original Kryptonian name.

Jason Lee – Pilot Inspektor
My Name Is Pilot Inspektor doesn't have the same ring about it

Bob Geldof and Paula Yates – Fifi Trixibelle, Peaches and Pixie
And their half-sister is called Tiger Lily.

David Duchovny and Téa Leoni – Kyd
Which just sounds like you can't remember your child's name.

Sylvester Stallone – Sage Moonblood
The *Rambo* star had to get 'blood' in there somewhere.

Gwyneth Paltrow and **Chris Martin – Apple** and **Moses**
Gwyn apparently chose her daughter's name because apples are wholesome, crisp and sweet.

Steven Spielberg – Destry
Possibly named after the James Stewart movie *Destry Rides Again*.

Angelina Jolie and **Brad Pitt - Shiloh Pitt**
The Rev. Spooner would have a field day!

Forest Whitaker – Sonnet, True and **Ocean**
Explaining the last two, he said; "I want those names to be their destiny, for my daughter to be honest and my son to be expansive. I try to be like a forest, revitalizing and constantly growing."

The Edge from U2 **- Blue Angel**
Maybe he's a Marlene Dietrich fan.

Frank Zappa – Moon Unit and **Diva Thin Muffin**
He also had Dweezil and Ahmet but, to be fair, Dweezil's birth certificate says Ian and he insisted on legally changing it himself.

Michael Jackson – Prince Michael and **Prince Michael II**
He's written hundreds of original songs but it seems the pop king was all out of ideas when it came to his kids.

Jermaine Jackson – Jermajesty

Seems the Jackson family have an obsession with royalty – and ideas above their station!

Bottom line

A mum who was six months pregnant was undressing in the bathroom when her three-year-old came in.

"Mummy, you are getting fat!" said the little girl.

"Yes, honey," replied Mum. "Mummy has a baby growing in her tummy."

"I know," said the girl. "But what's growing in your bottom?"

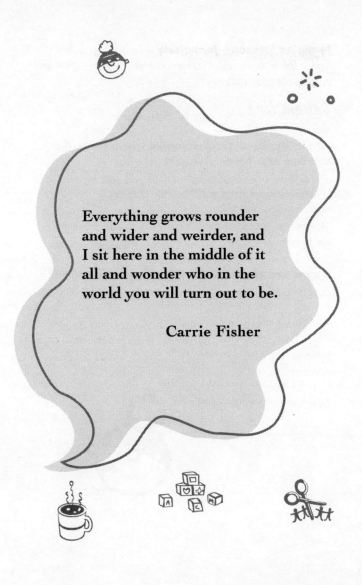

Everything grows rounder
and wider and weirder, and
I sit here in the middle of it
all and wonder who in the
world you will turn out to be.

Carrie Fisher

Thought for the day

A clean house is the sign of a wasted life.

If your dishwasher doesn't work, divorce him.

Life's a bitch – so you'd better become one.

The first thirty years of being a mum are always the hardest.

Marry Mr Right, as long as his first name isn't Always.

Never bake puddings – 'stressed' is 'desserts' spelt backwards.

You can fool some of the people all of the time, and all of the people some of the time, but you can't fool Mum.

Behind every successful mother is a basket of dirty laundry.

We'd all be perfect mothers, if we weren't so busy looking after kids.

Don't get mad; go shopping!

Housework can't kill you,
but why take a chance?

Phyllis Diller

Mother Madonna

Gwyneth Paltrow credits Madonna with getting her out of post-natal depression following the birth of second child Moses.

The Oscar-winning actress had 'a long wine-soaked dinner' with her popstar pal, where Madonna imparted her life-enhancing wisdom. "She is one of the most caring women and then she's also a very tough woman... She's very wise and she has a very soft, soft side.

"She really helped me out of my post-natal depression. I had a very interesting talk with her one night... She was very wise about life's bigger picture and when obstacles come up in our life it's for a very specific reason – they're there to teach us something that we haven't learned yet.

"She kinda made me see that my post-natal depression was an opportunity for me to change certain things about the way I was living and the way I was going forward.

"She really sort of reorganised my molecules in that situation."

I wish my parents had spent more time worrying about my education than me being a star.

Shania Twain

I BLAME THE PARENTS

There are plenty of things that kids, other people, teachers, policemen, the law courts, the government and just about everyone else will blame on 'the parents'. Now that you are about to become a parent yourself, you are descending into the 'blame zone'.

Whatever your child does and, once he or she has uttered his or her first words (something that you will yearn for for ages but may later, occasionally, wish had never happened), whatever your child says will be blamed on you.

This only applies, of course, to the overloud, rude, idiotic or otherwise embarrassing things your child does or says. If he or she does or says something incredibly intelligent it will be a case of, "What a clever child." For anything else it will be, "I blame the parents..."

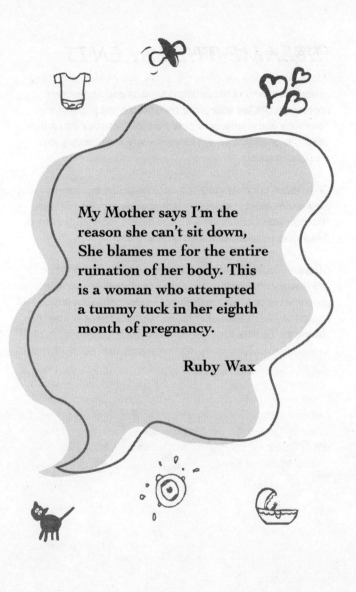

My Mother says I'm the reason she can't sit down, She blames me for the entire ruination of her body. This is a woman who attempted a tummy tuck in her eighth month of pregnancy.

Ruby Wax

Oops, I did it again!

When Britney Spears went off the rails, shaving her head, losing custody of her two children and ending up in a psychiatric ward, Lynne Spears naturally blamed herself. "As a mother, don't we always blame ourselves?" she said. "I took a lot of the blame. I took all the blame. The personality I have, it's always my fault."

Given that second daughter Jamie Lynn announced she was pregnant at 16, she may have a point. But Lynne admitted, on a talk show in the US, that she thought her youngest was joking when she broke the news – by writing a note.

"It said she was pregnant and everything was going to be OK. She was going to raise it... I thought it was a joke. I was waiting for the punch line," said the stunned mother. "I was in shock. I think I was just truly in shock, and then I started to cry. And she started consoling me at that point." Jamie Lynn gave birth to a girl in June 2008 and is raising the baby with her boyfriend in their Mississippi home.

Lynne's overwhelming feeling of guilt, however, didn't stop her writing a memoir about her life with her darling daughters – revealing that Brit, former Mouseketeer and one-time mascot of the 'Save it for marriage' crowd, lost her virginity at 14. Thanks, Mum!

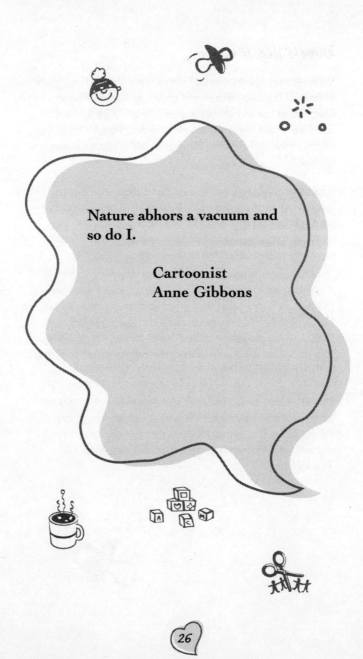

Nature abhors a vacuum and so do I.

**Cartoonist
Anne Gibbons**

Family portrait

When asked if she would like to have children, actress Drew Barrymore seemed confused about her family. "Definitely! I would like to have at least two, because I didn't have a brother or sister growing up," she replied. "I mean, I have a brother but we didn't really spend a lot of time together. And I have a sister too! S***!"

In fact, she went on to explain, she had never met her sister. "So you can see how close the family is. My family is awesome, but if you look up dysfunctional in the dictionary, there's our family portrait. Except it's all pasted together because no one was ever in the same room at the same time."

Sibling rivalry

Brother and sister Del and Nicola were having one of their everyday spats at home, while Mum was in the kitchen. Frustrated by her older brother, Nicola threatened to tell her mum what was going on. "Go on, then," said Del. "She's been my mum longer that she's been yours!"

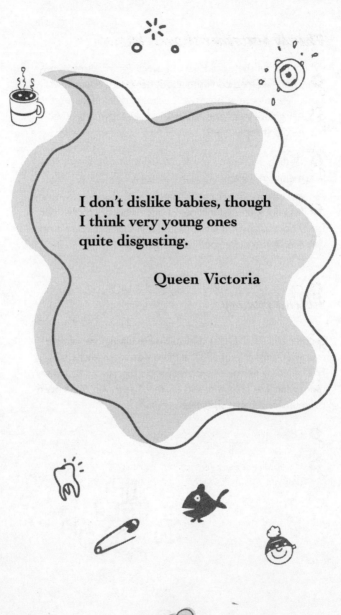

I don't dislike babies, though
I think very young ones
quite disgusting.

Queen Victoria

Things a mother should know

- Weetabix sets like cement in twenty minutes.

- Baby food can travel a remarkably long way when flicked from a plastic spoon.

- Getting dressed up to go out and then cuddling the baby is a big mistake.

- Orange baby food will NEVER come out of a white outfit.

- Babies always wait until you have left the room to perform their first roll – straight off the sofa.

- Older children will wait until you've left the room before shouting "Mummy!"

- It's a short step from the joy of hearing the first 'Mummy' to hearing it forty times a day.

- No matter how well you scrub the seats, the smell of baby sick stays in a car for weeks.

- Punctuality is a thing of the past.

- "I slept like a baby" is the most ridiculous phrase ever – unless it means "I woke up every three hours screaming!"

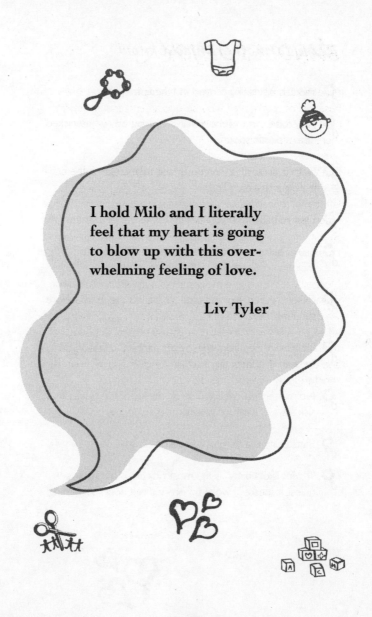

I hold Milo and I literally feel that my heart is going to blow up with this overwhelming feeling of love.

Liv Tyler

BUNDLES OF JOY

Nine months of waiting is over and the little darling is finally here. Life as you know it has come to an end and, while you have gained the glow of motherhood, you soon realise that there are a few drawbacks.

The things that used to mean so much to you, like making sure that your make-up and hair were just right before you left home, choosing the right outfit for the right occasion – perhaps even changing several times before you were happy with it – and carrying essential grooming aids in your handbag, are of diminishing importance.

More vital is checking to make sure that there's no baby food smeared on your face or in your hair, that whatever you are wearing is relatively free of baby puke and that your handbag – by now the size of a medium suitcase – contains enough of the right kind of cleaning wipes, spare nappies, bottles, food and changes of clothes that you will need to survive even the shortest foray into the outside world.

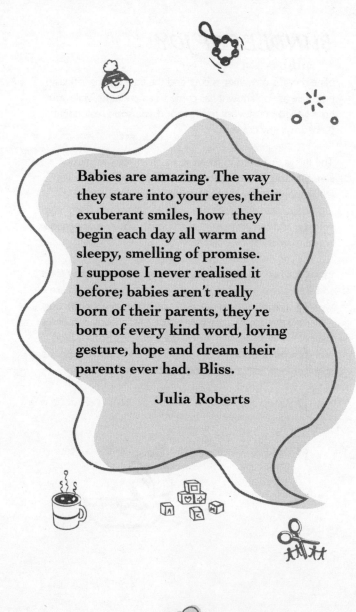

Babies are amazing. The way they stare into your eyes, their exuberant smiles, how they begin each day all warm and sleepy, smelling of promise. I suppose I never realised it before; babies aren't really born of their parents, they're born of every kind word, loving gesture, hope and dream their parents ever had. Bliss.

Julia Roberts

You know there's a baby in the house when...

🎵 The neat freak has abandoned the radiators and backs of chairs to wet washing and the clothes horse is permanently up in the living room.

🎵 The former style queen is still in her pyjamas at midday and hasn't combed her hair.

🎵 Hubby crawls out of bed in the morning with bags under his eyes and walks out the door without putting his trousers on.

🎵 The dog is no longer the main cause of rotten smells.

🎵 A romantic meal or a night out with the girls needs to be planned two months ahead.

🎵 There's nothing in the fridge and planning an evening meal feels more daunting than a hike up Mount Everest.

🎵 Stepping outside the front door requires more preparation than a polar expedition.

🎵 The word 'sleep' prompts more yearning than a naked picture of Brad Pitt.

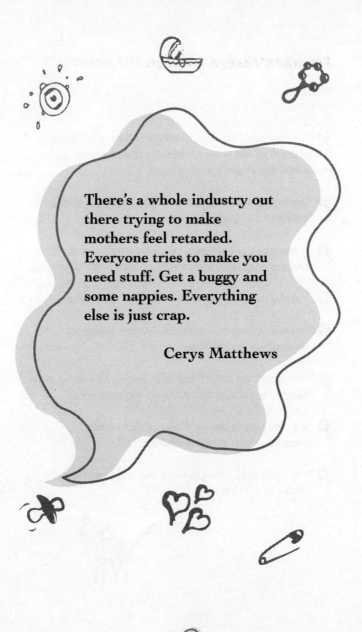

There's a whole industry out there trying to make mothers feel retarded. Everyone tries to make you need stuff. Get a buggy and some nappies. Everything else is just crap.

Cerys Matthews

Frequently asked questions

Q: Should I have a baby after 40?
A: No, 40 children is enough.

Q: I'm three months pregnant. When will my baby move?
A: With any luck, right after he finishes college.

Q: What is the most reliable way to determine a baby's sex?
A: Childbirth.

Q: My doctor says it's not pain I'll feel during labour, but pressure. Is he right?
A: Yes, in the same way that a tornado might be called an air current.

Q: Is there anything I should avoid while recovering from childbirth?
A: Pregnancy.

Q: Our baby boy was born last week. When will my wife begin to feel and act normal again?
A: When he goes to college.

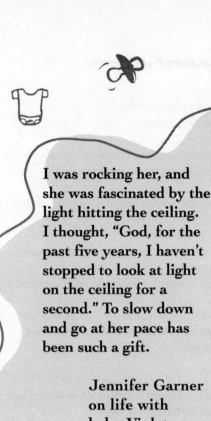

I was rocking her, and she was fascinated by the light hitting the ceiling. I thought, "God, for the past five years, I haven't stopped to look at light on the ceiling for a second." To slow down and go at her pace has been such a gift.

Jennifer Garner
on life with
baby Violet

And baby makes three...

Shortly after having her third child, Suzanne braved a trip to the local shopping centre. She bundled her two boys, aged four and two, into the car and put her baby girl in the car seat. The shopping done, she put the car seat on the ground in the car park while she strapped the boys in. Then she loaded her shopping into the boot, got into the car, and drove off. It wasn't until she got halfway down the road that she remembered the baby, racing back to find her still fast asleep in her seat, blissfully unaware of being abandoned by her mother.

Scary stats

A US study of parents with children under two found that by the time baby reaches his second birthday, he will have had 7,300 nappy changes.

Mums take an average of two minutes and five seconds to change a nappy (the equivalent of three 40-hour work weeks every year). Dad only take one minute and 36 seconds.

Mothers of pre-school children spend an average of 2.7 hours a day on primary childcare, while dads spend 1.2 hours – but at least they change the nappy faster!

Free the child's potential,
and you will transform him
into the world.

**Nursery pioneer
Maria Montessori**

Record-breaking mums

The wife of Russian peasant Feodor Vassilyev gave birth to 69 children between 1725 and 1765. In total she had 27 pregnancies which included 16 sets of twins, seven sets of triplets and four sets of quadruplets. Wonder if she lived in a shoe?

The oldest mum on record is Romanian Adriana Iliescu, who gave birth to a baby girl in 2005. She was 66. Adriana, who had nine years of fertility treatment to conceive, told the press before her caesarean section that, "If this child is born, it is also by the will of God."

Strangely enough, the Romanian Orthodox church didn't believe that God had anything to do with it and called her actions 'selfish'.

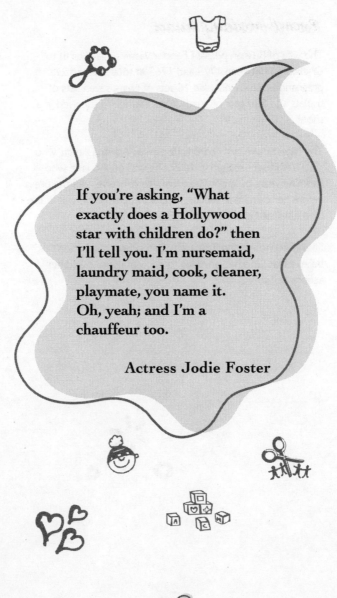

If you're asking, "What exactly does a Hollywood star with children do?" then I'll tell you. I'm nursemaid, laundry maid, cook, cleaner, playmate, you name it. Oh, yeah; and I'm a chauffeur too.

Actress Jodie Foster

Record-breaking babies

The heaviest newborn to survive was born to Italian mum Signora Carmelina Fedele in 1955. The baby boy weighed an eye-watering 10.3kg (22lb, 8oz). Ouch!

With a combined weight of 1,385g (3lb 0.8oz), Peyton – 585g (1lb 4.6oz), Jackson – 420g (14.8oz) and Blake – 380g (13.4oz) Coffey are the lightest triplets to survive. They were born by emergency caesarean section at the University of Virginia Hospital in Charlottesville, USA on November 30, 1998.

The threesome spent four months in hospital, with Peyton discharged first on March 12, 1999, followed by Blake on April 3, and Jackson on April 9.

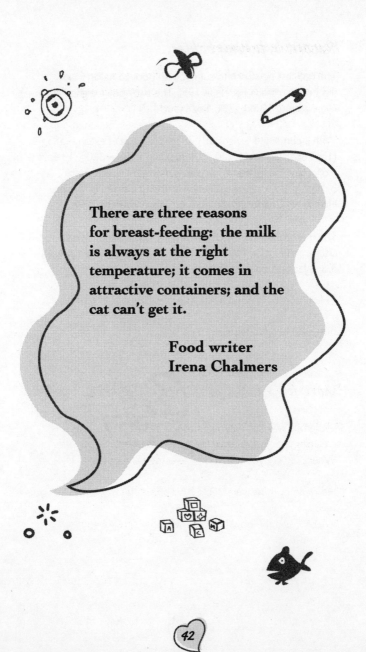

There are three reasons for breast-feeding: the milk is always at the right temperature; it comes in attractive containers; and the cat can't get it.

Food writer
Irena Chalmers

Favourite funnies

A pregnant woman is hit by a car and falls into a coma. Six months later she comes round and is told that the doctor has safely delivered her twins. "Your babies are fine," the doctor says. "You had a boy and a girl and your mother has been looking after them."

"What did you do about names?" she asks.

"Your brother named them for you," explains the doc.

"Oh, no, not him! He's an idiot! What did he call them?"

"Well, the girl he called Denise."

"That's not too bad. It's a nice name. What about the boy?"

"He called him De-nephew."

More funnies

A little boy was fascinated by his new baby brother who was screaming the house down for the fourteenth time that day. "Where did we get him from?" he asked his mother.

"He came from heaven," replied his proud mum.

"WOW!" said the boy. "I can see why they threw him out!"

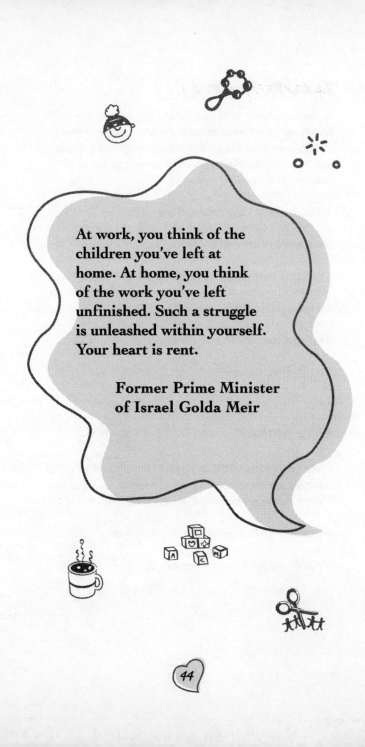

At work, you think of the children you've left at home. At home, you think of the work you've left unfinished. Such a struggle is unleashed within yourself. Your heart is rent.

Former Prime Minister of Israel Golda Meir

HAVING IT ALL

Thanks to feminism and equality laws, the majority of mums are also going out to work, either full or part time. In the UK 56 per cent of mums who have children under five work. That figure rises to 71 per cent for those whose youngest is between five and ten and 77 per cent whose youngest child is in the 11–15 age range. Figures are similar in most European countries and in the US 72 per cent of mums with children over the age of one are working.

In the past fifty years the workplace has adjusted to suit mothers with young children and many employers are flexible and understanding about the pressures they face. But having it all is not always easy, and the task of juggling baby and boardroom comes with many a pitfall.

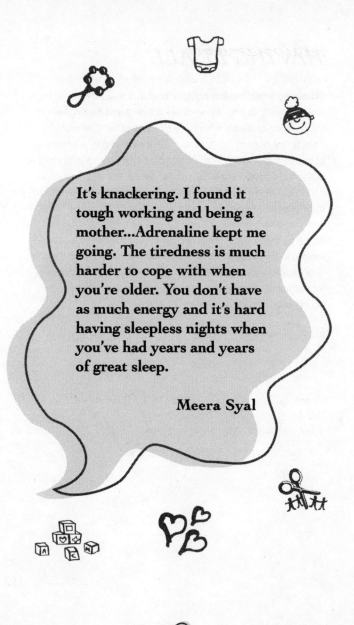

It's knackering. I found it tough working and being a mother...Adrenaline kept me going. The tiredness is much harder to cope with when you're older. You don't have as much energy and it's hard having sleepless nights when you've had years and years of great sleep.

Meera Syal

Perfect presentation

Laura ran her own successful PR company and, after six months on maternity leave, she decided it was time to go back to work. In the first week, she scheduled a meeting with her most important client to talk through their plans for the coming months.

After dropping her daughter off at the nursery, she got on a train to London, went straight to her meeting and gave a fantastic presentation to a boardroom full of high-powered men and women.

Afterwards, they chatted and they all seemed thrilled with her ideas and her plans for their leading campaign. Pleased with the outcome of the meeting, she went back to her office to tell her colleagues the good news.

As she came in the door her secretary looked slightly embarrassed and said, "Laura, have you seen the back of your jacket?"

Mystified, Laura took off the black jacket of her designer suit, and discovered a long white streak of baby sick all the way down the back!

Children learn to smile from their parents.

Japanese violinist and teacher Shinichi Suzuki

48

Guilt trip

Even the most glamorous job can't always erase that home/work dilemma. British actress and presenter Terry Dwyer admits that juggling a TV career with looking after son Caiden leaves her feeling 'permanently guilty.'

"I think that's the job description of a parent, isn't it?" she says. "The production team on *60 Minute Makeover* are really considerate about the fact I have a little boy.

"I do, however, feel that I see my driver more than my husband. I have a very good relationship with Bill, who's seen me breastfeeding in the back of the car!

"That's because sometimes I can take Caiden on set. We've even had some white overalls made for him!"

School sports

A six-year-old told her teacher that her mother wouldn't be able to watch her at sports day because she was too busy at work. "I'm sure she would be here if she could," said the teacher sympathetically. "She would much rather watch you than go to work."

"No, she wouldn't," replied the little girl. "She fancies her boss!"

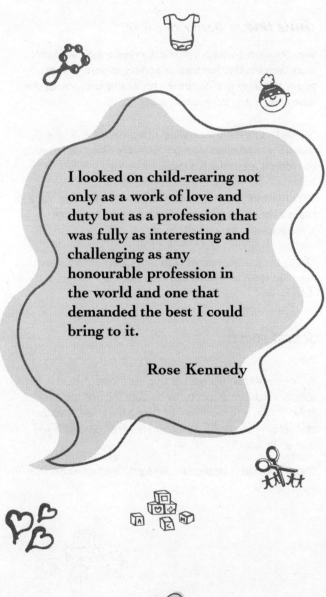

I looked on child-rearing not only as a work of love and duty but as a profession that was fully as interesting and challenging as any honourable profession in the world and one that demanded the best I could bring to it.

Rose Kennedy

Some things never change

As working mums have become the norm, men have had to share responsibility for childcare and housework. But when things go wrong, it seems it's still Mum who's more likely to put family first.

In a 2007 study by the University of Cincinnati, 813 working women and 599 working men were asked who would be the most likely to take time off work in the event of a child's sickness, failed childcare arrangements or school closure. A staggering 77.7 per cent of the women said it would be them, while only 26.5 per cent of the men said they would take time off.

Class act

Having met an important business contact at a corporate event, Jenny suggested they swap details. As the contact had no cards, she reached into her handbag to pull out a pad and then fished for a pen. Pulling out the only one she could find, she discovered it was not hers but her seven-year-old daughter's – a pink pen topped with a pink fluffy ostrich attached to a spring!

Another working mum was mortified in a meeting when her handbag tipped over on the floor and out fell a pair of her three-year-old's dirty knickers.

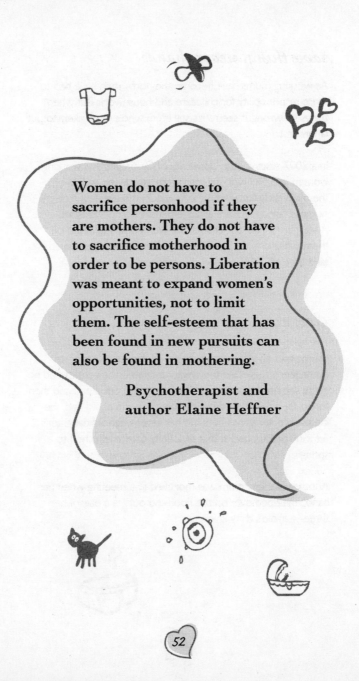

Women do not have to sacrifice personhood if they are mothers. They do not have to sacrifice motherhood in order to be persons. Liberation was meant to expand women's opportunities, not to limit them. The self-esteem that has been found in new pursuits can also be found in mothering.

Psychotherapist and author Elaine Heffner

Advertiser's dream

Maggie was worried her daughter was watching too much TV, but was often so busy with work she was pleased that her two children were at least quiet while she worked on the home computer. Her worst fears were realised when her nine-year-old daughter was in the bath and called out that she had run out of her usual conditioner. Maggie got her own bottle of a well-known brand out of the shower and gave it to Georgia who announced, in a perfect American TV accent, "It's professional but affordable!"

Mum's Army

A recent British report suggests that mothers who choose not to work are boosting the economy in other ways. Mums with young children carry out more than 173 million hours of community work each year, saving the Government almost £1 billion. As well as organising events, they care for the elderly and help in school. They also raise funds for charity to the tune of £133 million every year.

The study, commissioned by supermarket chain Tesco's Baby and Toddler Club, found that 68 per cent of stay-at-home mothers helped their local community for at least two hours a week and 58 per cent worked on a voluntary basis for ten hours a week. By contrast, 26 per cent of working mothers helped their community.

Right now, I spend all day
at home with my children.
Sometimes I become
Gwyneth Paltrow for a day
and put on make-up.

Actress Gwyneth Paltrow

Value for Mummy

A 2008 study found that the work of a UK mother was worth a salary of £29,000 a year. Researchers broke down the work needed to run the average housework and then calculated how much a professional would be paid to do the same. For example, for the 4.55 hours they spent getting children ready for school, taking them and collecting them, helping with homework and putting them to bed, a nanny would charge £36.40 a day. A further 71 minutes a day was spent cleaning and vacuuming, for which a cleaner would earn £7.10, and 14 minutes making beds, which would net a chambermaid £1.29.

An average of 14 minutes a day shopping would earn a professional shopper £2.10, while the 63 minutes she spent preparing food and cooking would earn a chef £17.30. Then there's the washing-up (28 minutes) for which a kitchen assistant would be paid £2.57, and dealing with the family finances (39 minutes) which would earn an accountant a very respectable £12.50. Then there's mum's taxi, in use for 23 minutes a day at a cost of £2.53.

All these added together came to a healthy wage of £29,771.56 – and that's without overtime.

Cleaning your house while
your kids are still growing is
like shovelling the sidewalk
before it stops snowing.

Phyllis Diller

SOCIAL PARIAH

Going out in public can be a hazardous pursuit when you have children. No matter how well you've trained them, they have the capacity to say and do the most embarrassing and inappropriate things just when you want them to be perfect.

As a special half-term treat, Heather and John took their two children, aged seven and four, to Disneyland Paris. After many a meal in themed cafes and burger bars, the couple decided they would splash out on an expensive French restaurant to round off the holiday.

The whole family dressed up and they soon found the most exclusive spot in the area, a lovely venue with starched white tablecloths and wonderful French food. The starter came and went and then came the main course…

Everyone seemed to be enjoying their food except four-year-old Joe, who was picking at his sausages with a strange expression.

"Eat up, Joe" Heather said. "You've got to finish the sausages or they'll be no dessert."

"I don't want them," moaned the little boy.

"Come on, eat them up," insisted Mum, at which point Joe opened his mouth and ejected a torrent of vomit, all over the posh white tablecloth, his own clothes, his mother's lap and the floor!

The waiters appeared from every direction and proceeded to mop up the mess with more pristine white linen tablecloths and a very sheepish family were left to apologise profusely to all the neighbouring tables and beat a hasty retreat.

Daddy's pride and joy

Helen was very amused to hear her four-year-old announce to Grandma that; "Daddy's got a big widdler!" Daddy wasn't so amused – and turned a deep shade of red.

What's that smell?

Mother-of-two Joss invited a couple of friends, and their children, round for a girly lunch. The three ladies sat happily chatting in the garden while their children played together.

After a while, Joss went in to get some more coffee and noticed a strong smell in the living room. Thinking someone's nappy needed changing, she checked all the youngest children, but to no avail. Her friends, Kath and Sam, looked around but found nothing.

It wasn't until the guest were leaving that the source of the stink became clear. In the open top of Sam's designer handbag, nestling on her mobile phone, Kath's two-year-old daughter Kady had deposited a perfect poo!

Disney disgrace

The first trip to a cinema was something of an uncomfortable affair for singer Cher.
"When I was four, my parents took me to see Dumbo and I was never quite the same," she once recalled. In fact, she was so taken with the whole experience that she deliberately peed in her seat so she wouldn't miss a thing.

Leno vents his spleen

Talk show host Jay Leno has always known how to make an entrance.

"One night in New Rochelle, my parents were having what I thought was a huge party, but I guess it was just two other couples over playing bridge," he recalls. "I'd gone up to bed, but I'd crept back to the top of the stairs to eavesdrop on the party below.

"They were talking and laughing and having a good time, and I wanted so badly to be down there where the action was. So I hatched a plan; I would make a big showbiz entrance! I would slide down the banister in my pyjamas, hit the bottom, land on my feet, and go, 'Ta-daaaa!' Right in the middle of the bridge game! I'd be the life of the party! Cause a sensation! Be like Liza Minnelli – who, of course, would have been about eight at the time, but still no doubt a load of excitement.

"So I balanced myself on the top of the banister and slid approximately one inch. And that was it. Suddenly, I fell like a nuclear missile – straight through a table with a lamp on it. There was a huge crash as the table collapsed and the lamp shattered.

"Everybody jumped up from the card game, scared out of their minds. But what an entrance! My parents rushed me to the hospital, where my spleen had to be removed. Which was so cool to me at the time – well worth giving up an insignificant body part. I've never really missed my spleen, anyway."

A thoroughly wet day

On a rainy summer's day, Karen decided to take her three kids to the local bowling alley with a friend. As they finished their game and prepared to go for a meal, three-year-old Harriet, stood up and peed all over the floor of the bowling lane. Horrified, Karen whipped her off to the loo and had to take her wet knickers off and stick them in a carrier bag. Having decided they would go for a pizza after bowling, Karen didn't want to let everyone down, so she took Harriet, now wearing a short dress and no pants, to a nearby shop and bought more knickers.

The party moved on to the restaurant, where they all ordered their meal and chatted over drinks. Suddenly Harriet crawled on to her Mum's lap for a cuddle and Karen said, "Aah, she must be getting sleepy." At which point the little angel had another pee, which soaked through her dress and drenched her mum!

Until I got married, when I used to go out, my mother said goodbye to me as though I was emigrating.

Actress Thora Hird

Vitamin sufficiency

Little Thomas had been given regular vitamin tablets and, being the chewy orange ones, he rather liked his tablets. One night at the dinner table, he had had his daily dose and knew he wouldn't be allowed another that day.

"Mummy," he asked earnestly, "Can I have another tampon after I've had a sleep?"

Logical View

Visiting a historical landmark, six-year-old Sam saw the plaque giving details of the building and a similar one next to it with braille writing on it.

"What's that for?" he asked his mum.

"That's for blind people, so they can read about the history of the building, too," she replied.

Puzzled, Sam looked around a little bit and then asked, "But how will they know it's there?"

Toddlers are more likely to
eat healthy food if they find
it on the floor.

Author Jan Blauston

Ten facts about shopping with the kids

1. No matter how many times they go to the loo before leaving the house, they will want to go again when you have a half-full trolley in the supermarket.

2. Even the shortest trip requires more luggage than a week away with Paris Hilton.

3. Any trip to ANY shop will result in the constant cry of, "Can I have…?"

4. In shops, children lose the ability to understand the word 'No.'

5. Surrounded by a wealth of goodies to choose from, they'll want to spend their pocket money on the one thing you really don't want them to have.

6. You will inevitably spend more than you intended on them.

7. Your teenage daughter will try on every pair of jeans/ party top/ pair of shoes in every shop in the shopping centre, before choosing the first one she tried.

8. However much you buy them, they will never have enough.

9. Your toddler will choose the most publicly humiliating spot in which to have a screaming tantrum.

10. You'll be so keen to get the trip over and done with that you'll forget half the things you went out for.

I am fond of children –
except boys.

Lewis Carroll

Love song

One day when she was just four years old, Jennifer Love Hewitt disappeared while eating in a hotel restaurant. "We were at a Mother's Day brunch and she wandered off," her brother Todd later recalled. Fortunately, her worried parents soon found her – on the stage in the dance hall.

"We heard this tiny little voice," Todd remembered. "We go into the next room and she's up on the piano singing a song that she heard on the radio."

The song? "Help Me Make It Through The Night".

First impressions

Sally was looking forward to having lunch with a new friend who had invited her round to her house. The lunch was beautiful and Sally was impressed at how immaculate the house was. As the two women sat and chatted, Sally's baby son Adam crawled around until, realizing he had escaped the living room, she went to find him. To Sally's horror, Adam's nappy had disintegrated and the hallway of the beautiful house was strewn with the jelly-like substance from inside, which now resembled deposits of frog-spawn. A mortified mum changed his nappy as quickly as possible and fled.

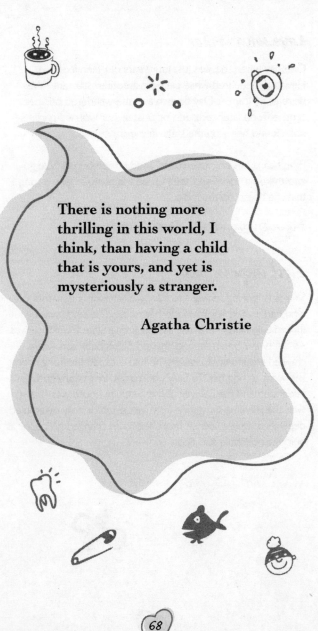

There is nothing more thrilling in this world, I think, than having a child that is yours, and yet is mysteriously a stranger.

Agatha Christie

Birthday blooper

Theresa's husband and daughter had arranged a surprise birthday party for her and invited all her best friends. As she was cutting the cake, her five-year-old son blurted out to one of her friend's husbands that he was "very grumpy". To make matters worse, he then added: "My mum said so."

Theresa has never been so embarrassed in her life. Luckily everyone, including her friend's husband, found it funny.

I can't believe he said that!

Eight-year-old Dominic was at a party with his parents and the children were playing games. In one, they sat in a circle and were asked questions. If they didn't get the right answer, they had to complete a dare or forfeit.

One little girl was told she had to kiss the person next to her. She looked at the little boy next to her and said, "I'm not kissing him." Instead, she puckered up and planted a kiss on the girl to her left.

"Ooh, look," said little Dominic, to the horror of his parents, "a bit of lesbo action!"

A mother's arms are more comforting than anyone else's.

Diana,
Princess of Wales

No so cute now

As Rod and Krystyna enjoyed an al fresco meal in France, a middle-aged French couple on the next table were clearly taken with their baby son. As Krystyna bounced him on her knee, she encouraged him to wave at the friendly pair, and they laughed and cooed with delight. The older couple's cute little poodle was not so impressed with the baby.

Finally, the lady asked if she could hold the baby for a little while. Krystyna willingly handed him over and he sat happily on the lady's knee – then chucked up on the floor at her feet. Rod and Krystyna were hideously embarrassed ... as were the French couple when their poodle darted out from under the table and ate up the vomit.

Well done, Mum

Two-year-old Matilda was being potty-trained and found the whole process a fascinating experience. If she joined her mum in the cubicle of a public toilet, she would ask (loudly, of course) whether it was a 'wee wee' or a 'poo poo' Mum intended to do. As if that wasn't bad enough, she would then clap and cheer when Mum began to pee.

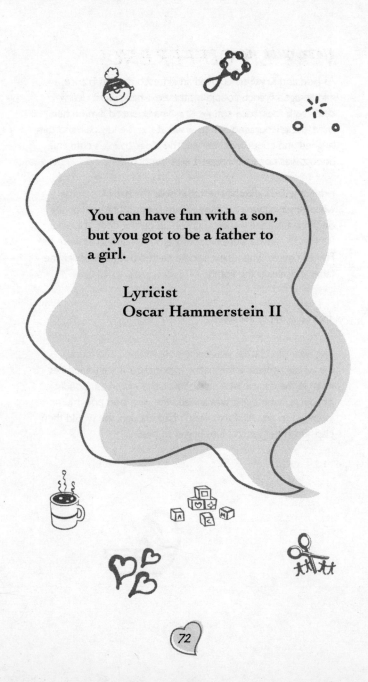

You can have fun with a son, but you got to be a father to a girl.

Lyricist
Oscar Hammerstein II

VIVE LA DIFFERENCE

Whether it's nature or nurture, by the time they are school-age boys and girls are not just a different gender; they might as well be a different species.

Girls come home from school with pristine shirts while boys have holes in trousers and clothes stained beyond the capabilities of the best washing powder. Give a boy a stick and it instantly becomes a gun. A girl will use it to make a fairy wand or a flag.

The gulf between the sexes remains a mystery that may never be solved. The one thing they all have in common is that they love their mums, and we love them both the same.

A girl is a person who screams at the mouse and smiles at the wolf.

Author Shyam Kapoor

Fashion victim

At the age of four, Gwyneth Paltrow's daughter Apple loved dressing up, and she made sure little brother Moses joined in too. "She makes [Moses] cross-dress," the Oscar-winning actress has said. "But she doesn't put make-up on him!

"My daughter plays with anything that's girly... She loves make-up," said Gwyneth, who is married to Coldplay frontman Chris Martin. "She puts on the eye shadow and my high heels. She likes to take my tank tops and make them a dress. And then she asks me to tie a rubber band on the back so they stay up.

"I don't like her to spray perfume on herself because she's so little, but she likes to spray it on me."

Mud monster

A despairing mum, watching her son come out of school covered in mud again, wailed, "Luke, why are you always so much dirtier than your big sister?"

With perfect logic, the little boy replied, "Because I'm closer to the ground than she is."

Boys are capital fellows in their own way, among their mates; but they are unwholesome companions for grown people.

Charles Lamb

Make tea, not war

Six-year-old Dylan was playing with his pal Joe. They had soldiers and all manner of weapons set up on and around a toy fort. Joe's mum then heard Dylan lay down the ground rules for the battle that was about to commence: "If you come near the castle I'll blast you with my guns, lasers, arrows and cannons. Except when I've invited you for a tea party."

Dictionary definition

Boy, n.: a noise with dirt on it.

Not Your Average Dictionary

Lending a helping hand

Louisa was getting a telling-off from her mum who scolded, "And I'll wipe that smile off your face, young lady."

"Don't worry, Mum," said brother Matthew, helpfully. "I'll do it."

Then he produced a tissue and began to scrub his sister's face.

There is not one female comic who was beautiful as a little girl.

Joan Rivers

Sugar and spice

Girls gossip
Boys shout

Girls spend hours trying to look their best
Boys take minutes to get covered in mud

Girls create
Boys destroy

Girls have tea parties
Boys have wars

Girls put on a show
Boys heckle

Girls think they know how everything works
Boys will take it apart to find out.

Boys say, "I didn't do it."
Girls say, "He did it."

Boys shoot from the hip
Girls shoot from the lip

Little girls are cute and small only to adults. To one another they are not cute. They are life-sized.

Margaret Atwood

Playmates

At his pre-school nursery, Alex had been best friends with a little girl called Niamh. A couple of years after they left to go to school, Alex and his parents were invited to an open evening with the other parents of former pupils. As they arrived they bumped into Niamh and her parents and Alex's mum said, "Alex, do you remember Niamh?"

The little girl looked at him expectantly but he said, "No."

"Oh, Alex," said mum. "You played with her all the time at nursery!"

"Oh, yeah, I remember," said Alex. "I didn't realise you were a girl!"

Pointed remark

Like most two-year-olds, Tilly's growing awareness of the difference between men and women meant she was fascinated with human anatomy. She would often point to at her Mum's chest in public and tell everybody that they were 'mummy's boobies'. One day, she excelled herself in a posh department store where she prodded a total stranger in the groin and declared, "Willie."

The man's girlfriend fell about laughing while an embarrassed mum pretended not to notice.

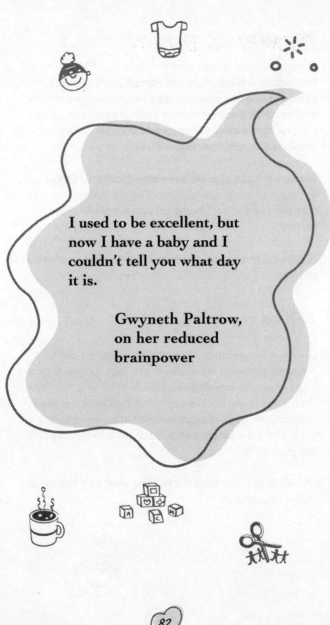

I used to be excellent, but now I have a baby and I couldn't tell you what day it is.

Gwyneth Paltrow, on her reduced brainpower

DUMBING DOWN

Pregnancy and childbirth have a way of turning your brain to mush, and sleepless nights that babies come with don't help. And by the time you get back to normal, with plenty of sleep and brain functioning perfectly, your children are old enough to make you feel stupid anyway.

Kids can make you feel like a moron even when it's them who are being dense. A mum who was lying in her bath one night remembered that the cat was still out, so she yelled to her six-year-old daughter, saying, "Halle, can you call the cat?"

A few minute later Halle knocked on the door, phone in hand, and said, "I can't. I don't know the number."

Boys wear their hearts on their sleeves. Even when they're trying to pull one over on you they're so transparent. Like men.

Patricia Heaton,
US actress and mother
of four boys

IT expert

On the home computer the task bar had moved to the side as a vertical column, instead of the horizontal bar across the bottom. Wanting to restore it, Dad spent twenty minutes looking through the settings and options in the control panel, but was flummoxed. Mum went through a similar rigmarole, going into all the setting controls she could think of, trying the tools – all to no avail.

Finally, Mum asked nine-year-old Georgia if she knew how the taskbar had moved and how to get it back in position. In an instant, she clicked on the bar and dragged it back to its intended place. Mission accomplished in two seconds flat, leaving a slightly red-faced Mum and Dad.

Spaced out

As her eight-year-old daughter Chloe was learning about space exploration at school, Annie explained that Neil Armstrong was the first man on the moon. Then she opened an encyclopaedia and showed the famous picture of the astronaut climbing down the ladder on to the moon's surface.

Chloe looked thoughtfully at the picture and then said, "If he was the first man on the moon, who took the picture?"

Like all parents, my husband and I just do the best we can, hold our breath and hope we've set aside enough money for our kid's therapy.

Michelle Pfeiffer

spelling bee

Caroline was proud that her four-year-old daughter was so great at spelling, so she loved to test her knowledge. One day they were sitting in the garden and she said, "How do you spell tree?" Sophie told her. "How do you spell dog?" Again Sophie answered correctly. "How do you spell cat?"

"Come on, Mum," cried Sophie in disgust. "You must know that one!"

show-off

Helen was sick of the other mums in her 'mothers and toddlers' group showing off about how clever their kids were. At one gathering, the most annoying of them started asking her one-year-old to point at various body parts.

"Where's your knee?" she asked, and he duly pointed. "Where's your head?" she continued and again he obliged.

For the following week, Helen trained her own toddler and, the next time the same mum started showing off her son, she went one better.

"Fred," she said sweetly, "Where's your larynx?" The tiny tot pointed to his larynx and went on to point out his vertebrae, his pelvis and his fibula.

Obviously, when you have kids, you realise nothing else is important.

Claudia Schiffer

Computer control

Five-year-old Sam asked if he could play on Mummy's computer, so she switched it on. As it was fairly slow to load, she told him firmly, "Until I tell you it's ready to use, DON'T TOUCH ANYTHING!" Off she went about her chores and forgot all about him.

Ten minutes later she heard a plaintive voice calling "Mum! Mum!" She rushed upstairs and into the study, where a patient Sam asked, "Can I touch my head?"

Who's the child here?

Part of the joy of parenthood is that you often find you have regressed to fairly childish behaviour yourself. When your children are old enough and smart enough to get the better of you in an argument, you may find your own grasp of language deserts you and end up uttering the following petulant phrases:

1. Oh, do what you like.
2. I don't care.
3. You are so annoying.
4. Because I said so.
5. I told you so.
6. What part of 'No' don't you understand?
7. I'm not listening!
8. I don't care who started it; I'm finishing it.
9. What did your last slave die of?
10. Whatever!

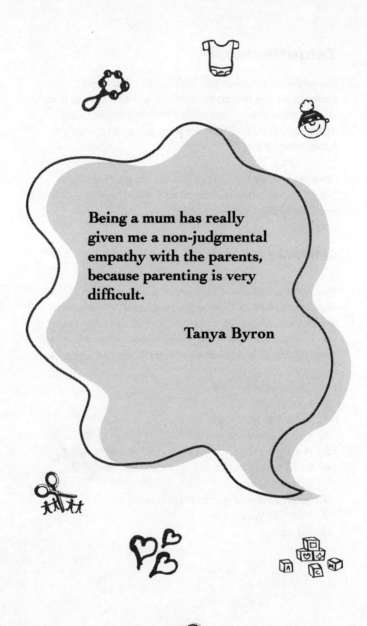

Being a mum has really given me a non-judgmental empathy with the parents, because parenting is very difficult.

Tanya Byron

Touché

Six-year-old Holly was playing with her mum's hair when she noticed a few strands of white. "Why are these hairs a different colour, Mum?" she asked. "Because every time you do something bad and make me angry, one of my hairs turns white," she replied.

Holly thought about it for a while and then gasped, "Wow! Grandma's hair is totally white. You must have been really bad when you were little!"

Growing fast

Four-year-old Jordan was having his hair washed in the bath when his mum said: "You hair grows so fast. I think you need another haircut!"

"Maybe," said Jordan earnestly, "you should stop watering it so much."

Sports nut

Four-year-old Edward pointed happily at the insect he had spotted in the garden and said, "Look, Mummy; it's a golf."

"No, darling," she replied. "It's a cricket!"

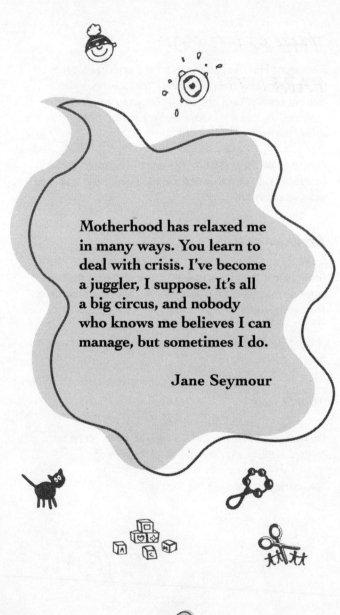

Motherhood has relaxed me in many ways. You learn to deal with crisis. I've become a juggler, I suppose. It's all a big circus, and nobody who knows me believes I can manage, but sometimes I do.

Jane Seymour

THE PERILS OF
PARENTHOOD

While every mother naturally regards her children as the most precious and rewarding things in her life, there are times when they can create a whole host of problems, some of which can be anticipated, but some of which take you completely by surprise.

Some would say that the little surprise packages, those innocent moments that seem to be going so well and then erupt into a complete nightmare, are what keep you on your toes: challenges that give you something to let you know that you can cope with just about anything. At times, though, they will floor you as effectively as a grand piano dropped from three floors up.

There are only two things
a child will share willingly
– communicable diseases
and his mother's age.

Dr Benjamin Spock

The birthday party

It's the day your little darlings wait for all year round, and most parents dread. You can spend months organizing the bowling party/disco/princess and pirate party and days beforehand making food, whipping up an impressive cake and wrapping 'pass the parcel' gifts, but when it comes to the big day, there are a few inevitabilities which every mother recognises.

1. At least 10 per cent of mums won't answer the invitation, leaving you either chasing them round the playground or playing a guessing game when buying paper cups and party bag fillers.

2. There will always be one child you'll feel like murdering by the time everyone goes home.

3. Among the many cheap plastic gifts, there will be one toy that doesn't work.

4. However indulgent you are on the day, the birthday girl or boy will be the one who ends up in tears.

5. You WILL have a headache at the end of the day.

If you bungle raising your children, I don't think whatever else you do well matters very much.

Jacqueline
Kennedy Onassis

Golden rules for buying birthday and Christmas presents

1. **Safeguard your sanity.** No matter how much your child begs for a set of drums or a voice-changing electronic toy, resist the temptation to indulge him.

2. **Minimise mess.** The idea of a card-making glitter kit or a set of beads is lovely, but the joy at the creativeness of your child will soon wear off when glitter and glue are trodden into your brand-new carpet.

3. **Think space.** Some of the huge plastic monstrosities on sale today will necessitate your moving house. Make sure you have the room first.

4. **Be prepared.** Always have a stock of various-sized batteries, especially on Christmas Day when the shops are shut, otherwise goodwill to all men, and especially parents, may soon disappear.

5. **Be a skinflint.** Don't go mad when they're young. Let's face it; two-year-olds have no idea how much you've spent on a toy and won't love it any more for it being worth a fortune. Save your money until they are old enough to fleece you properly.

As soon as you have a child, you can watch anything. We were watching Finding Nemo and I started crying so hard. Everything hits you more emotionally.

Actress Keri Russell

Pick of the bunch

Laura had just given her toddler, Caroline, a banana to eat.
Some time later, she noticed a small piece of banana on her
jumper and plucked it off. Being nowhere near the kitchen or
a bin, she did the next best thing and shoved it in her mouth,
only to find it was in fact a bogey.

Doctor nose best

In 2004, Innsbruck-based lung specialist Dr Friedrich Bischinger
claimed that picking the nose and eating it could be beneficial,
and told parents to encourage the habit.

"With the finger you can get to places you just can't reach
with a handkerchief, keeping your nose far cleaner," he said,
"and eating the dry remains of what you pull out is a great way
of strengthening the body's immune system. Medically it makes
great sense and is a perfectly natural thing to do.

"In terms of the immune system the nose is a filter in which
a great deal of bacteria are collected, and when this mixture
arrives in the intestines it works just like a medicine."

Eugh!

A baby will make love stronger, days shorter, nights longer, bankroll smaller, home happier, clothes shabbier, the past forgotten, and the future worth living for.

Author unknown

Pram panic

In the days when babies were often left outside in their prams, Maria put her baby daughter in the front garden while she went about cleaning the house. Popping out to check on her after a short while, she froze in horror. The baby, and pram, were gone.

Panicking, she ran up the street and turned the corner. Walking up the road was her five-year-old son, pushing a pram. He'd come home from a friend's house early and decided to take his little sister for a walk!

Indoor gardeners

Sarah was chatting to a friend in the kitchen while their toddlers played happily in the living room. Suddenly she realised that the children were very quiet and went to investigate. The troublesome twosome were sitting happily in the hall, scooping great handfuls of dirt from a potted plant and throwing it onto the stair carpet.

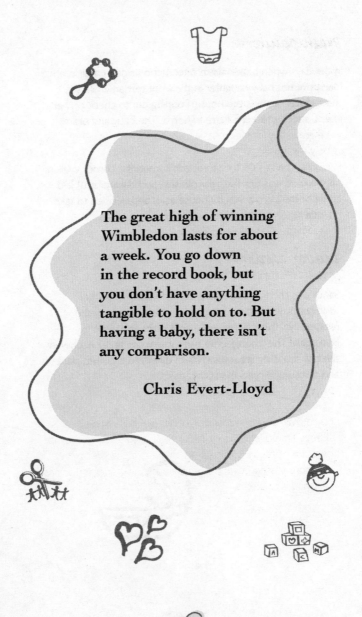

The great high of winning
Wimbledon lasts for about
a week. You go down
in the record book, but
you don't have anything
tangible to hold on to. But
having a baby, there isn't
any comparison.

Chris Evert-Lloyd

Night raiders

Amber asked her mum if her best friend could come for a sleepover and Sarah readily agreed. The two nine-year-olds had a lovely time together and went to bed quite late, around 10.30pm. Shattered, Sarah and her husband turned in about 11.00pm, after listening outside the door and making sure the girls were quiet.

The following day, Sarah went to the very high cupboard where she had hidden her secret stash of chocolate – which amounted to several bars - and there was not a square left. The sleeping beauties had crept out at 1.00am and scoffed the lot.

Family heirloom

While her husband was away on a business trip, Emma decided to invite some pals round for lunch, as well as their hordes of kids. The children were as well-behaved as expected for most of the day and, when it was time for them to leave, Emma breathed a sigh of relief that they hadn't trashed the place.

Having said goodbye to some of her guests, Emma heard a strange little cry, and rushed into the living room to find that one of the little girls had sat on an antique table, a family heirloom passed down from her husband's grandmother, and smashed it to pieces.

Sometimes when I look at all my children, I say to myself, "Lillian, you should have stayed a virgin."

Lillian Carter at the 1980 Democratic Convention, where her son Jimmy was nominated for a second term as US President

Careful what you wish for

Ten-year-old Claire came home from school one day and asked her happily married mother whether she thought she would ever divorce Claire's dad. Assuming her daughter was looking for reassurance, mum gave her a hug and said: "Of course not, darling. We love each other very much."

"Oh, I wish you would," said the petulant girl. "All my friends get twice as many presents and holidays as I do!"

Sorry, Mum, I forgot!

It's a familiar phrase to all mothers and, by the time you hear it, it's usually too late. They have arrived at school without that important permission slip, or have neglected to tell you that the teacher requested to see you – last week. For this Devon mum, it landed her in a very tight corner…

"I live in a little village and the local school kids take part in a club, a bit like a Sunday school, but on Wednesdays. One year they were putting on a Mother's Day mini-concert at the local church and all the kids were to perform some songs especially for the mums.

"My eldest daughter Jess was about eight at the time and I sat in the church proudly watching her recite poems and sing with the other children. Then the children sat down and a group of mums got up and walked to the front. A lady in the pew behind poked me in the back and said, 'You have to go up there now.' So up I went, thinking maybe they were going to give us a card or something.

"As I stood in line with the other mums and looked out at the congregation, I heard the first mum reading a poem about 'being a mum'. I looked down the line and realised to my horror that all the mums had a bit of paper with something to read out loud – except me, that is!

"I stood there racking my brains; 'Make something up', I told myself. I felt my face getting redder and wished that the floor would open up and swallow me. As the next mum began to read my mind went blank and I felt sick, this was worse than when my PE knicker elastic broke on sports day!

"The mum to my right began to read. I whispered urgently to the mum on my left, 'Miss me out; I have nothing to read.'

"'I have two,' she said, thrusting a bit of paper into my hand in the nick of time. I recited my poem and handed her back the paper. PHEW. My legs were still shaking as I got down from the stage.

"Later I asked Jess why she hadn't told me I needed a poem. 'Oh, yeah, I forgot,' she said.

"The moral of this story? Sometimes your kids forget to tell you really important stuff!"

Favourite funnies

Seven-year-old James was crestfallen when he came home from school one day. Concerned, his mum asked what was wrong. "We had a history test today," he said, "and I don't think I did very well."

"Why not?" asked Mum.

"All the questions were about things that happened before I was born," he replied.

In America there are two classes of travel – first class, and with children.

Robert Benchley

HOLIDAY HELL

As a mum, you can look forward to your child or children adding a whole new dimension to your annual holidays. You may want to share with them some of the places and experiences that were your favourites before the little darlings came along, and they will certainly bring an extra element of fun and excitement to all your usual holiday pleasures – but you can forget about ever luxuriating in the relaxing peace and quite you may previously have enjoyed.

Brigitte Bardot was on a skiing holiday with her parents when she was a teenager and her future husband Roger Vadim snuck into her room. When her father started banging on the door, the couple jumped into the snow, naked, from the second floor to avoid being caught.

Not everyone has quite such exotic tales to tell about their holiday experiences, but any mother who has ever taken her kids on holiday inevitably comes home with a story or two.

By and large, mothers and housewives are the only workers who do not have regular time off. They are the great vacationless class.

Anne Morrow Lindbergh, aviator and wife of Charles Lindbergh

Where's Molly?

Molly was four when she first went to France with her mum and dad, two older sisters and another family of five. The villa was beautiful, a huge stone building with round turrets at the top and only a ten-minute walk from the beach. There was a slight shortage of beds and, being the youngest, Molly ended up sleeping in a big iron cot, but she didn't mind because she was excited to be on holiday.

One day, the whole party of ten went down to the beach and had a lovely day in the sunshine. At the end of the day, some of the party made their way back to the villa while Molly's mum and dad stayed behind a little longer and then decided to pack up too.

Back at the villa, Molly's mum put the kettle on and pottered around the kitchen for while. It wasn't until she went to make the tea – Molly's favourite drink – that she noticed her daughter was missing. They'd left her on the beach!

The worried parents raced back down to the sand where they found a distraught four-year-old, surrounded by concerned French matrons and not understanding a word they were saying.

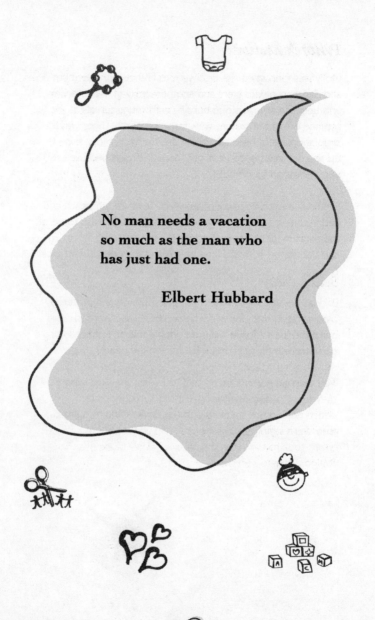

No man needs a vacation
so much as the man who
has just had one.

Elbert Hubbard

Fishy behaviour

On a family holiday in Spain, Gill and Maurice got friendly with another couple who were staying at the same hotel. One day on the beach, they were chatting as their children played and Maurice was slightly offended when new friend Mike suddenly jumped up, mid-conversation, and dived into the sea. However, this discourteous behaviour was soon explained when the man returned with Maurice and Gill's half-drowned five-year-old.

She had been trying, she explained, "to swim like a fish", despite being barely able to swim, and Mike had seen her hand waving above the water and dashed in to save her.

Beach baby

Joseph was five months old when he had his first taste of the Cornish seaside. Dad spread out a blanket on the sand and mum carefully placed him on his back in the middle. Not yet old enough to crawl, she figured he couldn't come to any harm there. Wrong!

Within seconds Joe had reached out his little hand, grabbed a generous handful of sand and dropped it straight into his open eyes. It took half an hour, and several bottles of expensive bottled water, to sort the poor mite out.

Wrinkles are hereditary.
Parents get them from
their children.

Doris Day

Cruising for trouble

Even the rich and famous can get it wrong when it comes to family holidays. Tom Cruise once took his kids away on a boating trip while his then-wife Nicole Kidman was filming *Moulin Rouge*. He hired a 40-foot fishing vessel and took seven-year-old Isabella and five-year-old Connor out on the Australian waters.

First, the motor conked out; then someone drove a Jet Ski into the boat's side and the vessel itself struck a reef. Finally, the barbecue flared up in Connor's direction and protective dad Tom chucked it over the side of the boat.

Back on dry land, Isabella summed up the trip for her mother: "It was tragic," she declared, "then fun!"

Christmas spirit

As a special treat for her children Charlie and Jessica, mum Lynn decided to splash out on a Christmas trip to Lapland where they could meet Father Christmas. Little Jessica was particularly excited and carefully composed a lovely letter to Father Christmas.

When they got to the Christmas grotto in Lapland, she let out an exuberant squeal and pointed. "Look, there he is," she told big brother Charlie.

"He's just a fat man with a beard," came the reply.

I curse my parents. I say to them, "It's your fault I'm single." They gave me such a great childhood.

Dannii Minogue

Tips for a stress-free holiday

1. Take car games, computer games and/or portable DVD player, to minimise the cries of "Are we there yet?"

2. Stock up with food for the journey, because there's some inexplicable connection in your kids' heads between travelling and eating.

3. Don't take games which are likely to end in arguments.

4. Take teabags, coffee and wine – by the time you reach your destination, you you'll need all three.

5. Take a book – if you're really lucky you might even be able to read it.

My mother could make anybody feel guilty – she used to get letters of apology from people she didn't even know.

Joan Rivers

6. Take an MP3 player and headphones; you don't even have to switch them on. That way you might be able to read your book in peace.

7. Don't look at the weather forecast before you go. It may well depress you.

8. Resign yourself to the fact that the sightseeing / spa treatments will inevitably be forfeited for theme parks and water parks.

9. Take your parents/in-laws. How else will you get a night out without the kids?

10. Leave the kids at home.

We are taught you must blame your father, your sisters, your brothers, the school, the teachers – you can blame anyone but never blame yourself. It's never your fault. But it's always your fault, because if you wanted to change, you're the one who has got to change. It's as simple as that, isn't it?

Katherine Hepburn

New shoes

Jack was two when his family went on a beach holiday. He soon found that he hated the feel of sand under his bare feet and, on the first day, refused to get off the beach towel to play with his big sister. The sandals his mum had brought were no help, because they simply filled up with sand and he hated that too. In exasperation, his mum left him with dad while she trudged a mile to a shop at the end of the beach and spent a fortune on a pair of sand shoes.

As she walked back towards her family, Jack was still refusing to leave the towel – until he caught sight of his mum. Then he jumped off the towel and ran to greet her, totally forgetting about the sand, which never bothered him again!

Fear of flying

In August 2002, a 12-year-old boy developed a flying phobia while on holiday in Ireland: not a problem if you happen to live in the UK, but his family had to get him home to Sao Paolo, in Brazil. His father spent thousands on hypnotism and tranquilizers to get him on a plane, but to no avail. Eventually he had to travel across land and water, finally sailing home from Genoa in Italy. The journey took twenty days.

French farce

Colin and Kirsty took their two boys, aged five and eight, on their first skiing holiday and booked them into ski schools at the French resort. On their first morning, they traipsed up to the meeting-place at the top of the mountain, where they discovered they were an hour late, because they had forgotten to change their watches to local time.

Spotting a group of kids of around Alex's age who were with an instructor nearby, they skied over and said to the French instructor, "Are you Jean-Pierre?"

"Oui," he replied.

Giving him Alex's name, they asked whether he was supposed to be in this class.

"Oui," he replied, and off Alex went.

Next they found a group that were around Edward's age and, after a similar exchange, left him there and went off for a morning of skiing.

On their return, at lunchtime, there was not a soul on the mountain. Slightly concerned, they skied to the other side of the mountain, where they discovered the meeting-place they should have gone to that morning, but didn't.

The ski school instructors were still there and Kirsty and Colin approached them and gave their children's names.

"They've been collected by their parents," said the instructor.

"No, they haven't," said Kirsty, panic setting in. "We're right here."

On second glance at the list, the instructor said, "Oh, no; sorry. They didn't turn up this morning."

By this time the couple were distraught, wondering where on earth their children could be. The instructor told them there was another ski school, situated on a completely different mountain, so they headed for that. To get there they had to take a ski-lift, a bubble lift and a cable car, as well as ski, and the whole journey took them two panic-stricken hours.

There they found the boys, sitting patiently in a glass waiting-room, hungry and cold but relieved to see them.

Their troubles weren't quite over, however. By the time they got down the mountain, the ski lift to their chalet had closed and they were forced to take a taxi all the way back at enormous cost.

If there were no schools to take the children away from home part of the time, the insane asylums would be filled with mothers.

US novelist
Edgar W. Howe

SCHOOL DAZE

The happiest days of your life? That's what school is meant to be for kids, isn't it? Was it the happiest time of your life? Sometimes we look back at our school days with an affection that has become warm and mellow over the years. The stresses we all face, of modern living, of high-pressure jobs and of having kids, all combine to make us forget that a child's schooldays can be not only the happiest time they ever have, but also their most stressful.

Peer pressure in the classroom and in the playground, as well as the worries about making sure that they don't let you down, can come to dominate a child's time at school and it's Mum's job to make sure that doesn't happen.

So when you're fretting over homework together, think of some of the stories here to remind you that it's not all as gloomy as it might seem.

Motherhood has a very
humanizing effect.
Everything gets reduced
to essentials.

Meryl Streep

Helping with the homework

Amy, the daughter of President Jimmy Carter, once brought a weekend assignment home from school concerning the Industrial Revolution. Stumped, she decided to ask her mum for help with the homework.

Mum Rosalynn was also clueless so, naturally, she asked a presidential aide to find out the answer from the US Labor Department. As the homework was due in by Monday, a notice to 'rush' was placed on the request.

A Labor Department official, thinking the request had come from President Carter himself, called in extra help and kept a full team of technicians and computer programmers working overtime throughout the weekend – apparently costing the taxpayer several hundred thousand dollars.

The resulting report was so lengthy that it was delivered to the White House by truck, but it managed to get there by Sunday afternoon, giving Amy plenty of time to finish the project.

Amy showed up the next day with the official answer to the question, but clearly her history teacher was not impressed. Amy's paper came back marked with a big red 'C.'

Every child is an artist.
The problem is how to
remain an artist once
we grow up.

Pablo Picasso

Is everyone paying attention?

On a school trip to a stately home, a teacher pointed out that the aristocratic family which owned the house was called Sydney and that there were had been several Philips throughout the generations. One had married a lady called Barbara and, in many of the sumptuous rooms carvings of the initials PS and BS could be found. In each of the rooms the teacher got the children to find the initials, repeating that they stood for Philip Sydney and Barbara Sydney. At the end of the tour the children were asked a few questions about the house.

"What do the initials PS stand for?" asked the teacher.

"Philip Sydney," replied one bright girl.

"And what does the B in BS stand for?" she asked, turning to a nine-year-old in the front. "Louis?"

Little Louis thought for a minute and then triumphantly declared, "Bob!"

129

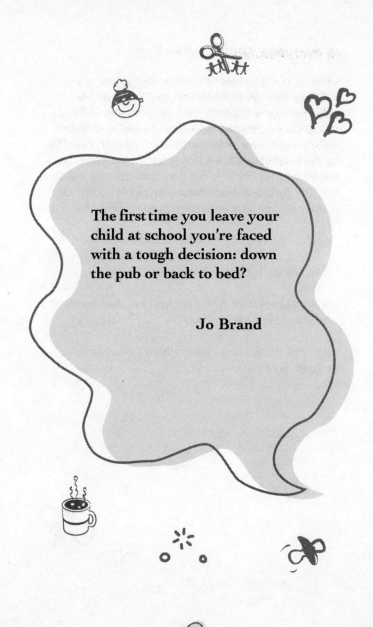

The first time you leave your child at school you're faced with a tough decision: down the pub or back to bed?

Jo Brand

Hi-tech heaven

Before he went to school, a mum decided her little boy should learn the Lord's Prayer. For a few nights he repeated it after his mum at bedtime until finally, she decided he could do it on his own. She was pleased to hear him recite the prayer perfectly right up to the last line. "And lead us not into temptation," he said finally, "but deliver us some e-mail, Amen."

Schoolteachers are not fully appreciated by parents until it rains all day Saturday.

Author E. C. McKenzie

Favourite funnies

A biology instructor at a girls' school asked a question of one of the young ladies in class.

"Miss Fortescue, can you name the organ of the human body which under the appropriate conditions, expands to six times its normal size, and describe the conditions?"

The pupil looked shocked and replied, "Sir, I think that is a most improper question. My parents will be most upset when I tell them this."

The teacher continued, asking another pupil, who replied, "The pupil of the eye, in dim light."

"Correct," said the teacher. "Now, Miss Fortescue, I have three things to say to you. One, you have not studied your lesson. Two, you have a dirty mind. And three, you will some day be faced with a bitter disappointment."

Simpson's school blunder

Pop star Jessica Simpson admits she was no boffin at school. "The first day of seventh grade, I was very nervous," she once recalled. "I was in history class and the teacher said to raise your hand if you know the continents."

Simpson raised her hand and... "I said, 'A, E, I, O, U!'

"Those aren't even consonants," Simpson helpfully pointed out. "They're vowels!"

Top marks

A female teacher was leaning across the desk marking a little boy's work. "Big ticks," the lad remarked.

Not quite sure if she'd heard properly, the teacher started checking her top to see if she was displaying too much décolletage.

"Pardon?" she asked.

"Big ticks," repeated the boy and, to her relief, she realised she was marking his work with bigger ticks than usual.

Just then a little voice piped up from the back of the class and said, "My mum's got big tits and she drives a bus!"

Playground Parade

While some mums turn up to the school playground looking like they've just stepped off the catwalk, others may look like they've just got out of bed – and probably have. The playground is a diverse and interesting place but, just to make it more amusing for you, here are the types you can look out for in a dull moment outside the school gate.

Yummy Mummy – The classic. She's good-looking, slim and well-dressed, her hair is well cut and her make-up expertly applied.

Klummy Mummy – She's got one up on the Yummy Mummy because she is the envy of the entire school run. She looks like a supermodel (i.e. Heidi Klum), has manicured nails, perfect hair and the latest in styles which would look, frankly, terrible on 99 per cent of mothers.

Chummy Mummy – Sensibly dressed, probably in a long skirt, she's the cheerful, giving type who can't wait to bound up to you in the playground and rope you into the school fete or Board of Governors.

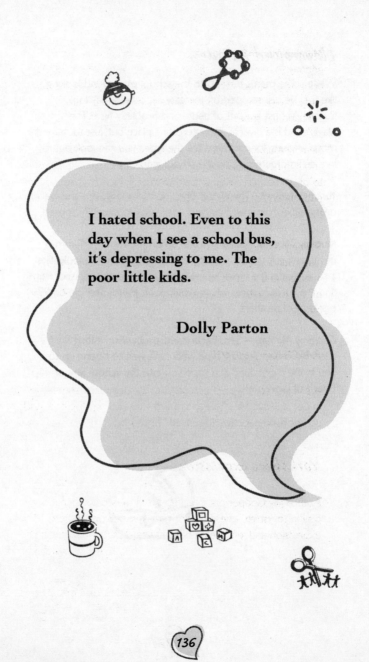

I hated school. Even to this day when I see a school bus, it's depressing to me. The poor little kids.

Dolly Parton

Mummy Mummy – The maternal type who devotes herself entirely to her children, always knows what her kids should be bringing to school and usually turns up twenty minutes too early to pick them up. She will be in jeans and boots, or a long skirt and flat shoes.

Slummy Mummy – This mum looks like she'd been slobbing about in her tracksuit bottoms all day but has barely had time to brush her hair. Just managed to drag herself off the sofa long enough to pick up the kids, but she'll soon be back in front of the telly.

Scummy Mummy – She might dress up a little for the playground, but it's bound to be inappropriate. A denim miniskirt and stilettos are her usual attire and she's likely to top off the look with a cigarette hanging out of one corner of her mouth.

Missing person

A primary school teacher asked her class to name something important that hadn't been around ten years ago. Victoria stuck up her hand eagerly and replied, "Me!"

Yorkshire expression

Author Jilly Cooper once related the "true story of a nativity play in Yorkshire, where the form master believed in free expression and left a team of eight-year-olds to write their

137

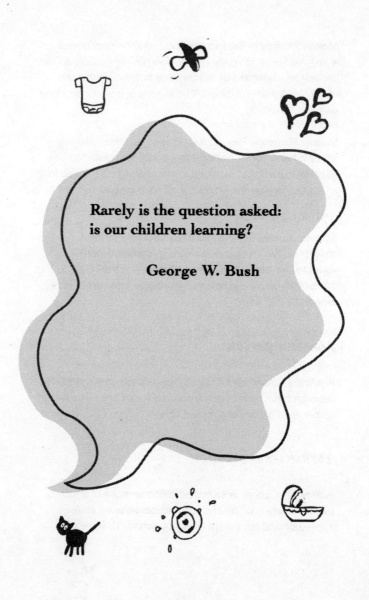

Rarely is the question asked:
is our children learning?

George W. Bush

own script and produce it themselves. The great day arrived, the hall was crammed with children, staff and doting parents. The curtains creaked back to reveal scene three, Mary in the stable. Enter Joseph with a briefcase.

Joseph: How's our little Jesus, then?

Mary: (after a long pause) He's been a right little booger all morning."

Pyjama mamas

School principal Joe McGuinness hit the headlines when he was forced to send a letter home to stop a worrying trend among parents – dropping their children off at school while still wearing their pyjamas.

The concerned head of St Matthew's School in Belfast politely pointed out that this habit set a bad example to pupils and made staff uncomfortable. As many as fifty women were gathering at the school gates in their nightwear every morning.

If you've never been hated
by your child, you've never
been a parent.

Bette Davis

The wonder of teenagers

They'll spend all their time worrying about the environment, and refuse to tidy their room.

They'll moan that there's nothing to do, and then stay out half the night doing it.

They're always broke, but never too broke for a night out or a ticket to a festival at a moment's notice.

They never want to talk to you but constantly accuse you of not listening.

They can talk for hours on the phone but fail to emit more than a grunt in your direction.

They're never hungry enough to sit down for a meal, but have plenty of room for bags of crisps and chocolate bars.

They can run rings around you when it comes to operating electronic gadgets, but have no idea how to make a bed.

They can spend hours in the bathroom, and still emerge looking like they just got out of bed.

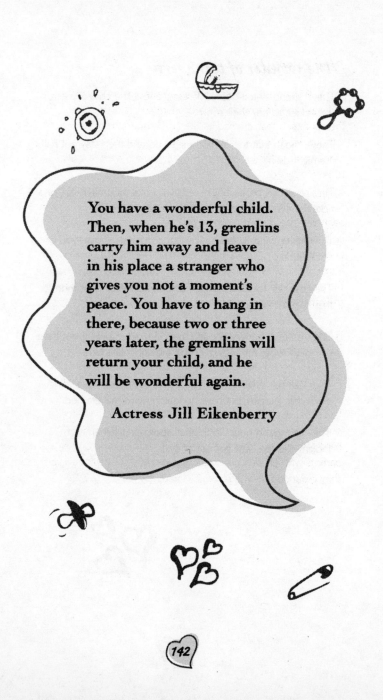

You have a wonderful child. Then, when he's 13, gremlins carry him away and leave in his place a stranger who gives you not a moment's peace. You have to hang in there, because two or three years later, the gremlins will return your child, and he will be wonderful again.

Actress Jill Eikenberry

Peer pressure

At 14, Abby was as sensible a teenager as you could wish for and was rarely in trouble with her mum and dad. One weekend she confessed that she had let the credit on her mobile phone run out, which was against the house rule that she always kept money on the tab for emergencies. As punishment, she asked to be grounded.

Knowing that she had been invited to a friend's birthday party, her parents were surprised and asked why she wanted to be grounded. Abby explained that the previous week there had been another birthday bash where the parents had been asked if their children were allowed alcohol. The mothers of two of the girls had said "Absolutely not" and the pair were ribbed by the other teenagers and felt left out of the whole party.

"I know they'll put me under pressure to drink," said Abby, "and I don't want to, so I'd rather not go. PLEASE ground me!"

"OK," said her rather proud mum. "You're grounded. No party."

Later that day, Abby was out shopping with her mum when one of her friends rang on her mobile phone. Mum could hardly believe her ears as Abby unleashed a diatribe on her 'evil' parents who treated her so badly, ending with: "I can't believe they grounded me! It's so unfair! I hate them!"

143

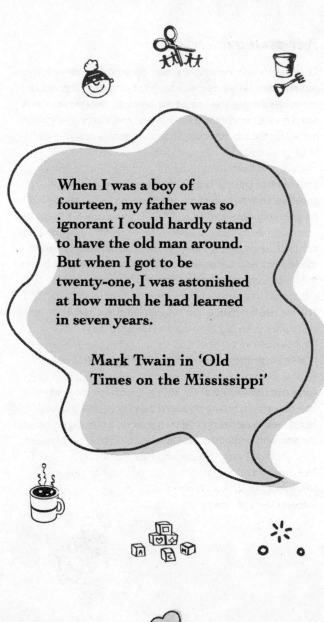

When I was a boy of fourteen, my father was so ignorant I could hardly stand to have the old man around. But when I got to be twenty-one, I was astonished at how much he had learned in seven years.

Mark Twain in 'Old Times on the Mississippi'

A teenage gift horse

On Julia's fortieth birthday, she was delighted to open a special present from her 16-year-old daughter. The generous lass, who earned a little every weekend working for a supermarket, had saved enough money to treat Julia and her husband to a night out at the theatre, watching *Chicago* in London's West End.

The pair had been clashing a lot in recent weeks, so the gesture was particularly touching. In a fit of gratitude, the proud parents agreed to let their daughter have a sleepover with two of her best friends.

On the evening of the show, Julia stocked the cupboard with snacks, fed the girls early, dolled herself up and set off with her husband to catch a train. They had a pleasant meal before the curtain went up and had a thoroughly enjoyable evening, catching the last train and arriving home at 1.00am.

As they opened the door, they were horrified to find several drunken lads in their living room with music cranked up to full volume. The house was trashed, empty beer cans and bottles lay all over the ground floor and food and drink were trodden into the carpets. Having thrown the lads out, the furious couple found their daughter upstairs in the bathroom, chucking up in the sink, with one of her friends asleep on their double bed.

Needless to say, their daughter was grounded for months and Julia learned to look a gift horse in the mouth – especially if there's a teenager involved.

Mother Nature is providential. She gives us twelve years to develop a love for our children before turning them into teenagers.

William Galvin

Help! I'm turning into my mother

Phrases you never thought you'd hear yourself say.

1. *That music all sounds the same to me.*

2. *That's way too loud.*

3. *I'm not made of money, you know.*

4. *Get off that phone! That call's costing a fortune.*

5. *You're not going out dressed like that.*

6. *Don't use that tone with me, young lady.*

7. *Wait 'til your father gets home.*

8. *It'll all end in tears.*

9. *Don't make me come up there.*

10. *For the third time…*

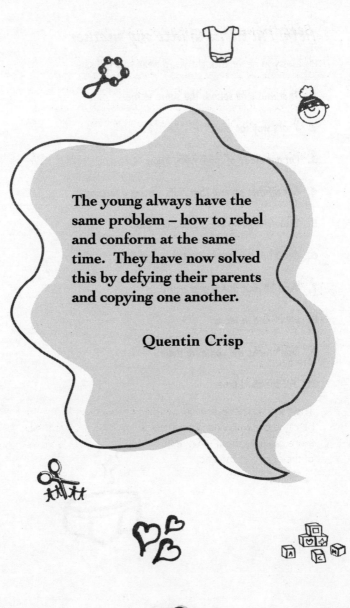

The young always have the same problem – how to rebel and conform at the same time. They have now solved this by defying their parents and copying one another.

Quentin Crisp

Beat them at their own game

Sick of their son's constant argumentativeness, and spouting of all the usual teenage clichés, Mike and Liz came up with a novel game. They listed the top ten phrases and split them into two groups, then put a chart on the wall which meant each of them scored points for the phrases on their list.

For example, Liz's list included:

1. That's SO unfair.
2. You're so embarrassing.
3. All my friends have got one.
4. Why do I have to do it?
5. You can't make me.

Mike's included:

1. I hate you!
2. You treat me like a kid.
3. Whatever!
4. I didn't do it.
5. It wasn't my fault.

Their son was soon so frustrated by their whoops of joy when he came out with one of their phrases that he began to think more carefully about what he said. Even he saw the funny side of their game in the end.

Children begin by loving
their parents; as they
grow older they judge
them; sometimes they
forgive them.

Oscar Wilde

Teen speak

As the dreaded teens hit, your sweet, articulate child will start by answering in grunts and then begin to speak a language you have never heard before. Here's a quick guide to what those peculiar creatures are saying to each other.

Bait – Obvious
Beverley Knight – A drink-fuelled evening – i.e. a night full of bevies.
Buzz – An attractive woman
Chirps – Chats up a member of the opposite sex
Cotching/Kotching – Chilling out
Dark – Horrible, gross or wicked
Devoed – Shortened version of devastated
Dry – Dull, boring
Flossing – Showing off and bragging about new or expensive clothes or items
Gantin' – Bad
Hench – Strong, as in muscular
Malt – Girlfriend
Nang – Brilliant
Neeky – Geeky
Rents – Parents
Safe Old – An adult who is considered to be OK
Tbh – To be honest
Yam – Eat

Mom and Pop were just a couple of kids when they got married. He was 18, she was 16 – and I was three.

Billie Holiday

Getting the message

A middle-aged mum has always been touched by the fact her son ended his texts and e-mails with the three letters LOL, assuming that it meant 'Lots of Love.' For some months she replied in a similar fashion until her embarrassed son finally explained to her that she was only supposed to add it when something was intended to be funny. It actually means Laughing Out Loud. Here's a quick guide to some of the most common text abbreviations:

AAF – As a friend

IMO – In my opinion

B/F – Boyfriend

G/F – Girlfriend

BTW – By the way

EOT – End of Thread (meaning end of discussion)

OTOH – On the other hand

G – Grin

BG – Big grin

VBG – Very big grin

LOL – Laughing out loud

ROTFL – Rolling on the floor laughing

H&K – Hugs and kisses

HAGD – Have a good day

IDK – I Don't Know

Soz – Sorry

ILU or ILY – I Love You

You know your child is a true teen when:

- She no longer wants you to tidy her room, although it's a total mess.

- He gets out of bed at noon and heads straight for the sofa.

- She stops talking to her friends the minute you enter the room.

- His room emits an unholy smell, even when you've cleaned it.

- The bargain clothes from the supermarket are no longer acceptable and only designer will do.

- His shirt is never tucked in when he goes to school.

- Her pocket money is spent exclusively on make-up.

- His walk begins to resemble a particularly lazy gorilla.

- She gives up all her hobbies and thinks exclusively about boys.

- He would rather chew coal than kiss his mother.

I'm trying to get stricter, to make my children behave better at meal times... but I am the original voice of no authority.

TV cook
Nigella Lawson

156

Holy order

Bruce Springsteen's mum had always set her heart on her son being an author and wasn't too happy about his desire to be a rock guitarist, so she sent him to see a priest.

"My mother – she's very Italian – she says, 'This is a big thing. You should go see the priest,'" he recalled. Bruce obediently knocked on the rectory door and told the priest, 'Hi, Father Ray, I'm Mr Springsteen's son. I got this problem. My father thinks I should be a lawyer, and my mother wants me to be an author. But I got this guitar...'

'This is too big a deal for me,' Father Ray replied. 'You gotta talk to God... Tell him about the lawyer and the author, but don't say nothin' about that guitar!'"

Rebel Spacey

It seems Californian actor Kevin Spacey was a difficult child. At the age of 14, his parents had had enough and shipped him off to a military academy in the hope of knocking some discipline into him. When asked, years later, what had prompted the move, he said: "I won't tell you exactly what the incident was that made my parents send me to military school. Let's just say it involved my sister's tree-house and some matches."

In America you're not allowed to talk about how motherhood is driving you crazy, or how you don't like it, or how, if you have to give a bath one more time, you're going to pull your hair out... You can complain about your job, your husband, your friends, but God forbid you complain about your kids.

Desperate Housewife Felicity Huffman

WAIT 'TIL YOUR FATHER GETS HOME

So you've read all the books and watched the TV programmes, but discipline still seems to be an issue. Let's face it, not everyone has Supernanny to hand and it's pretty hard to keep your cool when the kids are driving you crazy.

Take heart from in the fact that you are not alone. Mums all over the world are tearing their hair out at this very minute because even banishing their kids to the famous 'naughty step' halfway up the stairs is having no effect whatsoever on their rebellious monsters.

Never give in: simply accept that sometimes you just can't win.

My daughter has a problem picking things up in her room. So if she leaves her clothes on the floor, we put them in a bin bag. She has to earn them back by being tidy.

Madonna

Things you say ten times a day:

1. Rubbish belongs in the bin, not on the floor.

2. Turn that down!

3. Can you please put things away when you've finished playing with them?

4. Who spilled that?

5. Have you cleaned your teeth yet?

6. Did you flush?

7. You're the oldest; you should know better.

8. Stop hitting your sister.

9. Turn that light off!

10. Go to your room!

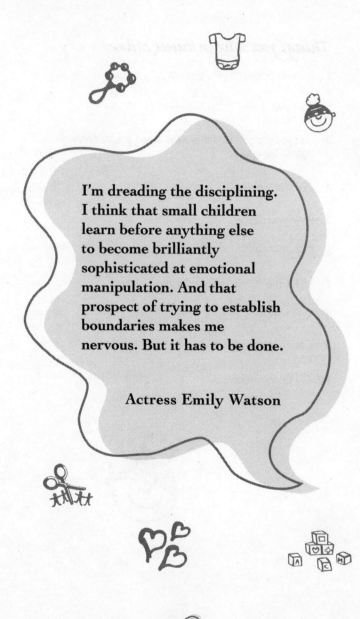

I'm dreading the disciplining. I think that small children learn before anything else to become brilliantly sophisticated at emotional manipulation. And that prospect of trying to establish boundaries makes me nervous. But it has to be done.

Actress Emily Watson

Things you'll hear twenty times a day.

1. I'm bored!

2. I'm hungry.

3. It wasn't me.

4. That's not fair.

5. You're so mean.

6. Puh-leeze, Mum.

7. Lauren's mum lets her...

8. In a minute.

9. Can we go home now?

10. He/she started it.

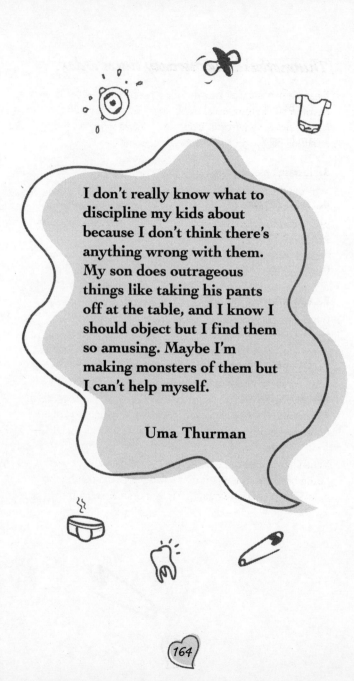

I don't really know what to discipline my kids about because I don't think there's anything wrong with them. My son does outrageous things like taking his pants off at the table, and I know I should object but I find them so amusing. Maybe I'm making monsters of them but I can't help myself.

Uma Thurman

The mother of invention

Dean Kamen is a well-known American inventor who has devoted his life to medical technology and also created the famous Segway Human Transporter – a two-wheeled, self-balancing platform on which the 'rider' stands.

At 16, he invented a control unit for light and sound shows and sold the product to such clients as New York's Hayden Planetarium. The young entrepreneur suddenly found himself with a considerable sum of money burning a hole in his pocket.

"I used some of the money to send my parents on a two-week vacation," he later recalled, although his apparent generosity had an almost inevitable ulterior motive, "and I used the rest of it to buy myself some really great machine tools for the workshop I had set up in my parents' basement."

Dean knew that the new equipment was far too bulky to take through the house and down into the basement in the normal way. Undaunted, ever inventive, and with his parents out of the way, Dean hired a builder to dig a huge hole in the garden and expand the cellar, knocking down a foundation wall of the house in the process.

When his parents came back from Hawaii, they found their house had been placed on stilts to prevent it caving into the hole. Kamen recalled simply, "They were not amused."

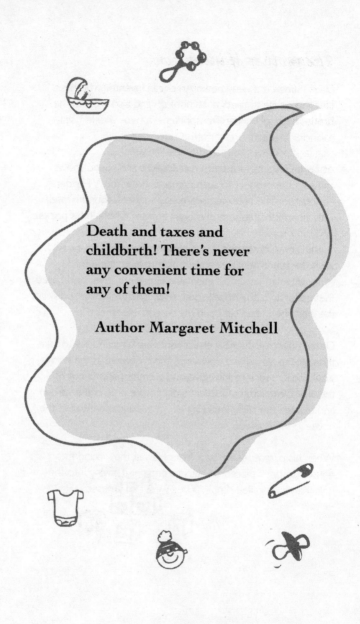

Death and taxes and childbirth! There's never any convenient time for any of them!

Author Margaret Mitchell

Lessons to be learned

Sharon Osbourne and rocker hubby Ozzy brought up their kids in a deliberately relaxed atmosphere, allowing them to do pretty much whatever they liked.

Son Jack, however, still had the need to rebel and ended up on drugs. In 2003, he went into rehab and is now clean.

"Rebel kids are crying out for discipline," Jack said in an interview with *The Times*. "When I was six, I was a maniac. We had motorbikes at our house in the country and I was always pushing my luck: crashing, lying winded and in agony for a bit, then doing it again. I was never going to learn my lesson."

Naturally, mum Sharon blames herself for the fact that he went off the rails.

"I don't blame the rock 'n' roll lifestyle. I blame me," she says. "You get caught up in the BS, and I did; 'Oh, your mom's really cool. She's really easygoing.' I should have had more boundaries. I should have had more structure for Jack."

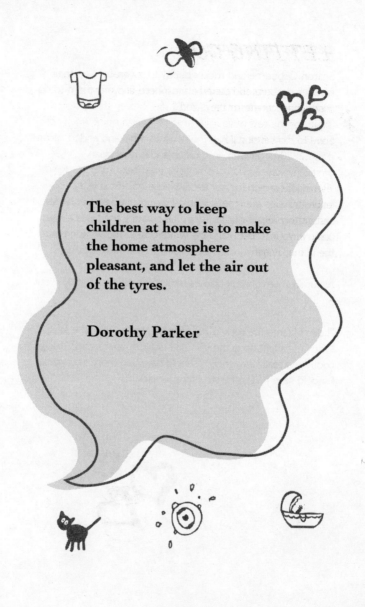

The best way to keep children at home is to make the home atmosphere pleasant, and let the air out of the tyres.

Dorothy Parker

LETTING GO

With every step, and every year, children find more independence and, much as you'd like to keep them in your sights for the rest of your life, there comes a point when you have to start letting go.

First they start to stay out all night, then learn to drive, start earning their own money and leave school. At some point, either through going to university, finding a job elsewhere or just getting their own place, you'll be waving them off with a lump in your throat – and possibly a bottle of champagne on ice in the kitchen!

A child's spirit is like a child; you can never catch it by running after it; you must stand still, and, for love, it will soon itself come back.

Playwright Arthur Miller

Advantages to empty nest syndrome

You'll finally have that spare room you always wanted –
even if you're still hoping it's usually filled with its
original occupant.

You get your TV remote back.

Foreign holidays cost less, and you can avoid everybody
else's screaming kids because you don't have to go in the
school breaks.

Food bills will drop dramatically without lumbering
teenagers raiding the fridge every five minutes.

You'll see less of the in-laws – they weren't popping round
to see you after all.

You can make mad passionate love to your husband any
time, anywhere – if you still have the energy and
the inclination.

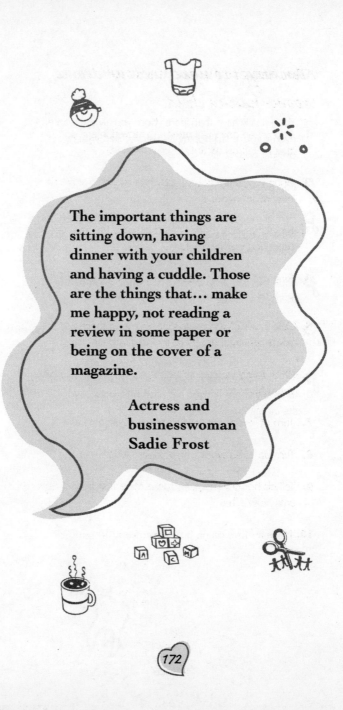

The important things are sitting down, having dinner with your children and having a cuddle. Those are the things that... make me happy, not reading a review in some paper or being on the cover of a magazine.

Actress and businesswoman Sadie Frost

Ten ways to embarrass your room-sharing child

1. Pop round one night after he's moved in and announce that he left his security 'blankie' behind.

2. Bring your collection of baby pics round to show his cool new room-mates.

3. Ring him every morning to make sure he's cleaned his teeth and washed his face.

4. Ring him every night to make sure he's going to bed on time.

5. Take a pair of your own slippers round there and tell him you're leaving them there for your frequent visits.

6. Offer to do his ironing, "because I know how you hate your undies to be creased."

7. Turn up every night with a home-cooked meal.

8. Turn up at his work with a packed lunch.

9. Tell his hot new (female) room-mate that he wet his bed until he was ten.

10. Make a move on his hot new (male) room-mate.

A mother becomes a true grandmother the day she stops noticing the terrible things her children do because she is so enchanted with the wonderful things her grandchildren do.

US author Lois Wyse

Crowded nest syndrome

As financial pressures on the young become more difficult to cope with, it seems more and more adults are opting to stay in the parental home well into their twenties and even thirties.

This increasingly large group have been nicknamed Kipper Kids in Parental Pocket Eroding Retirement Savings.

A survey published in July 2008 found that one in three parents in the UK (34 per cent) believed it was likely their children would be living at home until their mid-thirties and that figure rose to 43 per cent in London.

Investment provider Skandia polled more than 2,000 people and found that although most parents hoped their adult children would become financially independent (83 per cent) and would buy a house (63 per cent), many thought there was little hope of that happening.

Even if they left, 40 per cent feared they would still be clearing children's debts through adult life and those considered wealthy parents (those with a household income of between £50,000 and £100,000) were the most likely to fear the worst (44 per cent).

When grandparents enter the door, discipline flies out the window.

Ogden Nash

WHEN YOUR BABIES HAVE BABIES

Becoming a granny is one of the best perks of being a mum. You have the delight of having children around without all the hard work. When the babies cry you can hand them back, you don't have to clean up their mess every day and discipline is not your problem.

And you get to wreak revenge on your own kids for all the grief they caused you when they were growing up.

A grandmother is a babysitter who watches the kids instead of the television.

Author unknown

Turning the tables

🌸 If your grandchildren are staying over, let them stay up really late – they'll be hell to live with the next day.

🌸 Grannies are allowed to spoil, so make sure they are   filled with plenty of fizzy drinks and chocolate before they go home.

🌸 Take them to the park all day and then deposit them, cold, hungry and covered in mud, on their parents' doorstep.

🌸 Tell them lots of stories about what a naughty little girl Mummy was when she was growing up.

🌸 Take them to expensive shops and tell them to put what they want on their birthday list.

🌸 Give them a list of the numerous pets Mummy was allowed when she was little.

🌸 Buy them the noisiest toy you can find – or a drum kit.

🌸 Encourage them to make a lovely card for Mum, smothered in glitter and beads, then send it home with them.

If I had known how wonderful it would be to have grandchildren, I'd have had them first.

US author Lois Wyse

Favourite funnies

A little girl asked her Granny how old she was. Granny replied she was so old she didn't remember any more. Said the little girl, "If you don't remember you must look in the back of your knickers. Mine say five to six."

More funnies

When granny came to visit, little Jimmy was so pleased to see her, he ran up the path to hug her.

"I'm so glad you're here," said the little boy. "Now daddy will have to do that trick he said he would do."

"What trick is that?" asked a puzzled Gran, to which Jimmy replied: "He told Mum he'd eat his hat if you were ever staying in his house again!"

Granny nose best

Noticing that three-year-old Georgina had a nasty bogey sticking out of her nose, Granny went to get a tissue. When she returned she offered the tissue to the little girl, who declined the offer with the immortal line; "It's all right, Granny. I've pushed it back up!"

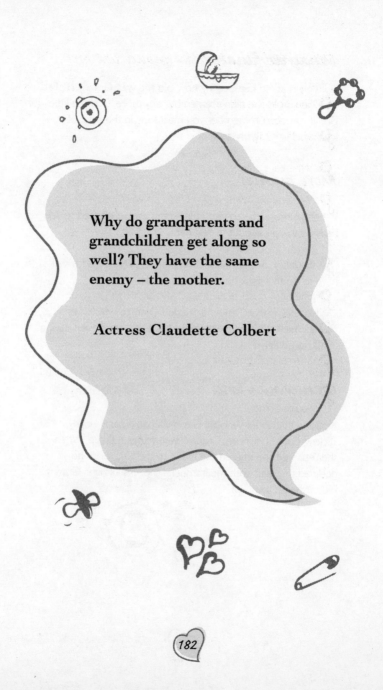

Why do grandparents and grandchildren get along so well? They have the same enemy – the mother.

Actress Claudette Colbert

What not to say to the proud parents

- She looks just like Grandad.

- That's not the way to hold him.

- When are you getting her ears pierced?

- Will you be having another one soon?

- That's the way we did it, and it didn't do you any harm.

- Shouldn't you be potty-training him soon?

- She's not quite as pretty as Laura's little girl.

- How much did the other granny spend on the gift?

- Shame she's got your ears.

- I'll only stay for a few weeks… just until you know what you're doing.

No matter how old a mother is, she watches her middle-aged children for signs of improvement.

Playwright
Florida Scott-Maxwell

ONCE A MOTHER...

You've willed yourself to let go, helped your kids to leave home and encouraged them to lead an independent life. No matter how well your kids are getting on, however, you will never stop doing what you're best at… being a mum.

The Mother's Day tradition

Although the huge industry surrounding Mother's Day is
a relatively new thing, the idea of having one day a year to
honour the woman who brought you into the world stretches
back as far as the ancient Greeks. They kept a festival to
Cybele, the mother of the Greek gods.

In ancient Rome a similar festival known as Matronalia was
held and, in honour of matriarchal goddess Juno, presents were
given to mothers.

In the UK, the tradition of Mothering Sunday is thought to
have started around four hundred years ago when, instead of
attending their local church, domestic servants were allowed to
attend services in their home village – their mother church. For
many this day, the third Sunday in Lent, was the only time that
the were reunited with their families. Consequently, 'Mothering
Sunday' came to refer to their reunion with their family more
than their sojourn to their original church.

As a gift to bring to their mothers, cooks would often bake a
cake, traditionally a Simnel cake, similar to a Christmas cake,
which laid the ground for the bearing of gifts on the day.

The phrase Mother's Day was coined by American campaigner
Anna Jarvis in 1912. She specified the position of the
apostrophe, making it a singular possessive, as she felt that it
should be about each family honouring their own mother, not
all the mothers of the world.

Anna, whose fight to enshrine a day devoted to mothers was prompted by the death of her own, was victorious in 1914 when President Woodrow Wilson passed a bill declaring the second Sunday in May Mother's Day: but Anna's idea was quickly hijacked and commercialized by big business, which horrified her. In protest she set up the Mother's Day International Association and tried to copyright the date, to which end she spent the entire family fortune and even got arrested for disturbing the peace during a demonstration. In 1948, she died in poverty.

Mother's Day is now celebrated in countries around the world, on many different dates, and is also a global industry.

In 2008, according to a US business researcher, Americans spent $2.6billion on flowers, $1.53billion on pampering gifts – such as spa treatments – and another $68million on greeting cards. Another $3.51billion went on dining out.

In the UK, it's the biggest day in the calendar for florists. In 2006, for example, orders included 3.7million mixed bouquets, 394,000 bunches of roses, 294,000 bunches of tulips, 293,000 bunches of freesias and 93,000 foliage plants.

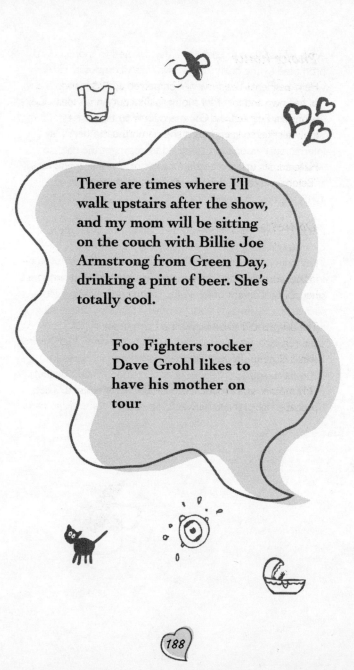

There are times where I'll walk upstairs after the show, and my mom will be sitting on the couch with Billie Joe Armstrong from Green Day, drinking a pint of beer. She's totally cool.

Foo Fighters rocker Dave Grohl likes to have his mother on tour

Phone home . . .

Halle Berry has been married and divorced twice, had a baby of her own and forged a successful Hollywood career, including winning a Best Actress Oscar win for *Monster's Ball*. But Mum Judy still likes to keep tabs on her famous daughter.

Halle admits that the best advice her mother has given her is, "Before you do anything life-changing, call me!"

Domestic goddess

Katherine Heigl might be classed as one of the sexiest women in the world but that doesn't stop her mum nagging her about her ability – or lack of it – in the kitchen.

The 30-year-old star, who married Josh Kelley in 2007, says she regularly gets a dressing down from her mum, Nancy, who thinks it's time she learned how to cook.

"My mother says I should cook more," Katherine says. "She's probably right. I think she wants me to be a domestic goddess."

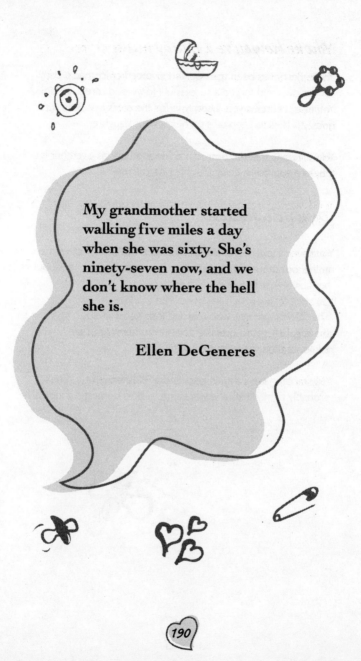

My grandmother started walking five miles a day when she was sixty. She's ninety-seven now, and we don't know where the hell she is.

Ellen DeGeneres

You know you're a clingy mum when...

You carry a picture of your grown-up daughter in your purse.

You insist he holds your hand to cross the road, even though he's 22

You still cook their favourite meals once a week, even though they're never there for dinner.

You'd rather move house than throw away the thousands of pictures they did as a child.

You haven't touched a thing in their room, even though they moved out ten years ago.

You start to sleep with their favourite childhood teddy bear.

You reject every boyfriend/girlfriend you meet because they're not good enough for your baby.

You start tagging along when they go to nightclubs.

Always be nice to your children because they are the ones who will choose your rest home.

Phyllis Diller